DATE DUE

GAYLORD			PRINTED IN U.S.A.

THE WORLD'S
GREATEST
EXPLORERS

THE WORLD'S
GREATEST
EXPLORERS

William Scheller

Foreword by Robert D. Ballard

illustrated with photographs and maps

The Oliver Press, Inc.
Minneapolis

Library of Congress Cataloging-in-Publication Data

Scheller, William.
The world's geatest explorers / William Scheller;
foreword by Robert D. Ballard

p.   cm. — (Profiles)
Includes bibliographical references and index.
    Summary: Relates the enterprises and discoveries of twelve explorers, including Vasco da Gama, Captain James Cook, and Roald Amundsen.
ISBN 1-881508-03-X : $14.95
1. Explorers—Biography—Juvenile literature.   [1. Explorers.]
I. Title. II. Series: Profiles (Minneapolis, Minn.)
G200.S44   1992
910.92'2—dc20   92-18418
[B]   CIP
                                                                 AC

ISBN 1-881508-03-X
Profiles III
Printed in the United States of America

99 98 97 96 95 94 93 92   8 7 6 5 4 3 2 1

Contents

Roald Amundsen and his party raised the flag of their country—Norway—upon reaching the South Pole in 1911.

Foreword

We tend to think that the era of exploration on Earth is over; that the last frontier left to explore is space. The youth of today are given the impression that unless they are one of the lucky few to become an astronaut they can never become an explorer. That all there is left to do on Earth is to fill in the small voids left unexplored in some distant jungle or a remote frozen ice cap.

Nothing could be farther from the truth. The vast majority of Earth remains unexplored. We now have better maps of Venus and the far side of the moon than of Earth itself.

Seventy-one percent of the planet lies underwater, the majority of which remains unexplored. There are more active volcanoes underwater, the largest mountain ranges on the planet lie there, and canyons far grander than the Grand Canyon are hidden in darkest reaches.

Given recent advances in undersea technology including the advent of sophisticated unmanned robotic systems, the next generation will explore more of Earth than all previous generations combined.

If this is true, and I believe it to be the case, it is critical that the next generation understand what exploration is all about, and what better way to do that than through the eyes of our most noted explorers. Men like Captain James Cook, Lewis and Clark, Peary and others.

Humans are born seeking answers to many questions. And one of the most fundamental questions asked is "Where am I?" Hopefully, this book will rekindle the flame of curiosity in many of its readers. A curiosity that can only be quenched by readers setting out on their own adventures. And as they set down this book and wonder, let them remember the words of an English writer from his poem "The Explorer":

"Something hidden. Go and find it. Go and look
    behind the Ranges—
"Something lost behind the Ranges. Lost and
    waiting for you.
Go!"
Rudyard Kipling (1898)

Robert D. Ballard, Director
Woods Hole Oceanographic Institution
Center for Marine Exploration
Woods Hole, Massachusetts

Introduction

*W*hat makes an explorer?

That's a hard question, with perhaps as many answers as there have been explorers. Perhaps we should ask instead, What makes human beings want to explore strange places? Why are we the most curious creatures on earth?

If the earliest humans were living in a place where no enemies bothered them and where they had plenty of animals to hunt and other food to gather, they stayed there. Why look for trouble somewhere else?

But if food became scarce or if neighboring tribes made trouble, early humans might look to other lands. Thus, the first explorers made their discoveries not because they loved to travel and learn, but because they wanted two important things: food and safety.

Later, when people had lived in one place for a long time with plenty to eat and little to fear from enemies, they had different reasons for exploring. Perhaps by traveling to distant places they could trade with other people and bring riches back to their cities. Or, if they were warlike, they might venture from their homes to conquer neighboring lands, seize treasure, and build great empires. Among some people, spreading their religious beliefs from one land to another became important. Very often, all these reasons worked together to send explorers to distant lands and seas.

Still, few people explored out of simple curiosity. Those who did were often thought strange by their friends and neighbors. Just like the earliest humans, the stay-at-homes thought, "Why look for trouble? Why leave home and family, except to become rich or power- ful or to spread the word of God?" Even as recently as the early days of our country, no one bothered to climb mountains, because no one thought that anything of value would be found on the mountain top.

About 300 years ago, however, things began to change. Of course, people still cared most of all about food and safety, and the power of their countries. But a new power was growing in the world—the power of science. More and more, people wanted to know about their world, not only for the power and riches it would bring, but also for the sake of knowing. This new kind of curiosity led to the greatest age of exploration in history. By the middle of the twentieth century, explorers had sought out the last undiscovered places on earth and had stepped into space.

The explorers in this book left their homes for many

reasons. Some, like the Portuguese sailor, Vasco da Gama, and the Canadian Alexander Mackenzie, opened up new routes for trade. Governments eager to expand their power and also to learn new things about the world, sent out other explorers, like Captain James Cook and the great team of Meriwether Lewis and William Clark. Still others, like the polar explorers Roald Amundsen, Robert Peary, and Matthew Henson, worked mainly to add to our knowledge of geography. Each of these explorers won for himself a lasting place in history.

These explorers, and others like them, did their work so well that people often say that the only place left to explore is space. Space, of course, is an exciting frontier. And the map of the earth has been filled in. But this does not mean that the job of world exploration is done. Even though people have been just about everywhere on earth, we still have much to learn about how land, water, and all earth's living things work together. For example, we are only beginning to find out how important the great rainforests are, and to discover the many kinds of creatures that live in them. We also need to know more about why deserts sometimes grow larger and spread into land needed for farming. And we still understand very little about the bottom of the sea. Explorers of the future will answer these questions, and more.

A strong sense of religious duty inspired the fourteenth-century Arab scholar Muhammad ibn-Batuta to begin his travels, which would ultimately cover more than 75,000 miles.

12

1

Muhammad ibn-Batuta

*N*ot all explorers travel to remote parts of the world, where perhaps no one has ever been before. One of the greatest explorers in history was a man who followed routes that already existed and went to places where there were already cities and palaces. His name was ibn-Batuta, and he lived in the Moslem world of 600 years ago.

Ibn-Batuta is remembered not for a single trip he took, but for a lifetime of traveling. Indeed, his life was one long exploration of his world. Also, like the great Italian traveler Marco Polo, he had a fine talent for looking sharply at anything he saw and for remembering it so he could tell about it later. Much of what we know about life in the places he visited, in his far-off time, comes from the stories of his travels.

Muhammad ibn-Abdullah ibn-Batuta was born in 1304, in the Moroccan city of Tangier on the Strait of

Gibraltar—the narrow body of water that separates North Africa from Spain. Although Morocco was his home, he really belonged to a much larger world. By the 1300s, all of North Africa, the Middle East, and southern Asia as far as India and Indonesia were united by belief in the Moslem religion, called Islam. Ibn-Batuta spent much of his life exploring this Islamic world.

Ibn-Batuta's earliest travels came about because of his Moslem religion. At least once in his life, every Moslem is supposed to visit Mecca, in Arabia. The pilgrimage to this holiest city of Islam is called the *hajj*. In 1325, after studying to be a lawyer like most of the men in his family, ibn-Batuta decided to make the hajj. For someone living 3,000 miles from Mecca, this was a big decision, since the journey would take a year or more. For ibn-Batuta, his pilgrimage was the beginning of a trip that would last 24 years!

The 21-year-old lawyer left Tangier in June 1325, and did not reach Mecca until October of the next year. Even in those days, 16 months was a long time for traveling 3,000 miles. But the places along the way, as well as the place where he was going, interested ibn-Batuta. He stopped for a while in Tunisia, on the north coast of Africa. Then, after crossing the Libyan Desert, he visited the great Egyptian cities of Alexandria and Cairo. At Cairo, and later at the ancient city of Damascus, in Syria, ibn-Batuta visited famous Moslem colleges and studied with learned men.

The Egyptian pyramids and Great Sphinx near Cairo still look much like they did when ibn-Batuta saw them more than 650 years ago.

Leaving Damascus, ibn-Batuta joined a caravan and crossed the fearsome Arabian Desert to reach the holy city of Mecca. (A caravan is a group of people who travel together by camel and on foot. This was how ibn-Batuta moved about through much of his life, and it is still the way some people cross the deserts of Africa and Asia today.)

Once he had made his visit to Mecca's holy places and performed his religious duties, ibn-Batuta made the greatest decision of his life. He would not go straight home to Tangier. Instead, he would keep traveling. Content with his choice, ibn-Batuta joined a caravan that was leaving for Baghdad, which is north of Arabia, in the land now called Iraq.

Ibn-Batuta was the sort of traveler who never went anywhere in a straight line, if there was anything interesting to turn his attention. He had heard about the beautiful cities of Persia (today called Iran) and went east to visit them before turning west to Baghdad. In Baghdad, he became friends with government officials, who invited him to go with them to other cities in Persia. Because of his good education and pleasing manner, ibn-Batuta was often able to meet learned and important people. They made traveling easier for him, and helped show him the glories of Moslem civilization in the places where it had been born.

By the time ibn-Batuta had finished touring Persia and Iraq, the season of year for the hajj had come around once again. Being a religious man, he went again to Mecca in 1327. Ibn-Batuta had now been away from home for three years, and he needed a rest. So, he decided to stay in Mecca for a year, studying and talking with other travelers, until the time came to continue his journey.

Up until this next adventure, ibn-Batuta had always traveled by land. Now he would take his first sea voyage, down the Red Sea between Arabia and Egypt. He headed for Yemen, at the southern tip of the Arabian peninsula. Beyond Yemen, a much larger sea stretched to the south. This was the Indian Ocean, which Arab traders sailed on their way to Asia and Africa.

16

In the time of ibn-Batuta, people did not simply decide when they wanted to travel and then make their plans with ship owners and caravan leaders. Travel was nothing like it is today, when ships, planes, and trains leave at regular, scheduled times. Hundreds of years ago, people and goods moved according to the season, instead of the clock. The great caravans would leave from Cairo and Damascus because the time of year for the hajj had come. Captains would sail their ships out into the Indian Ocean because it was the season when the winds blew in the right direction. And there was no way that ibn-Batuta could call ahead to arrange a place for himself on a ship. A traveler like ibn-Batuta had to go to a seaport and ask until he found a captain willing to take a passenger. He had to be ready to sail when the captain was ready.

That is what ibn-Batuta did in 1329. He traveled to the southern Arabian port of Aden. There he found a trading ship that was headed down the coast of east Africa. Ibn-Batuta was by now collecting places almost as one might collect stamps, and we can imagine how eager he must have been to see one of the most unusual parts of the Moslem world. When the ship reached Mogadishu, in what is now Somalia, and then sailed even farther south across the equator to the country we now call Tanzania, the young man got his first look at towns where most of the Moslems were black Africans. Islam, he must have been proud to see, had indeed spread far.

From Africa, ibn-Batuta sailed north again to Arabia

and by a zigzag route got himself back to Mecca in the year 1330. Mecca, by now, was for him more than a holy place. It was his favorite spot for resting and collecting his thoughts between trips.

And the trips grew longer and longer. His new plan was to sail to India, but he had trouble finding someone in Arabia who knew India and could go with him as a guide. So he decided to travel by land. Perhaps he would meet a guide along the way.

The land route ibn-Batuta chose began in Turkey, which he reached by sailing in a merchant ship on the

The Prophet Muhammad, founder of Islam, was born in Mecca about 570 A.D. Moslems still travel to the Prophet's Mosque to worship, much as ibn-Batuta did nearly seven centuries ago.

Thousands of Moslems gather to pray in Mecca at the Holy Kaaba, the holiest site in Islam and the chief goal of the Moslem pilgrimage. Wherever Moslems pray, they face in the direction of the Holy Kaaba inside the Great Mosque.

Mediterranean Sea. Here was yet another land and yet another kind of people, and once again the traveler's attention was turned. He wandered all over the Turkish peninsula, even taking side trips across the Black Sea to what is now the country of Ukraine (in the former Soviet Union) and to the great Christian city of Constantinople. This surely wasn't the quick way to India! But because ibn-Batuta took so much extra time, he was able to learn about a part of the world that was changing very quickly. The Turks were growing more powerful, and the empire of Constantinople—the

19

Ibn-Batuta often traveled by caravan across vast deserts.

Byzantine Empire—was growing weaker. In another 120 years, the Turks would conquer Constantinople, and it would be a Christian city no longer. Today, it is the Turkish city of Istanbul.

When ibn-Batuta finally pointed himself in the direction of India, he traveled along one of history's most famous trade routes. Since ancient times, the caravan roads across central Asia had been busy with traders carrying Chinese silks and spices from the Indies. Now, with his horses and camels, servants and friends, ibn-Batuta crossed the broad Asian plains and made his way through the mountain passes of Afghanistan. By September 1333, he was in India.

When he set out for India, ibn-Batuta already had a plan in mind. He had heard that the Moslem ruler, or *sultan*, of northern India liked to give important jobs to

learned Moslems from other lands, and ibn-Batuta felt he might be just the sort of person the sultan was looking for. Ibn-Batuta had been away from home for eight years. He was not a poor man to begin with, and during his travels, he had been helped with presents and gifts of money from rich people who felt it was their duty to help a traveling scholar. But by now, he probably wanted to earn money on his own. He had studied law and could work as a lawyer or judge anywhere where Moslem law was the rule.

Ibn-Batuta found what he wanted. The sultan, Mohammed Tughluk, asked him to become a judge. But he had to promise to stay at the capital city of Delhi. He did stay—for eight years. Toward the end of that time, however, he grew afraid of the sultan, a dangerous man who sometimes turned against his friends and officials.

21

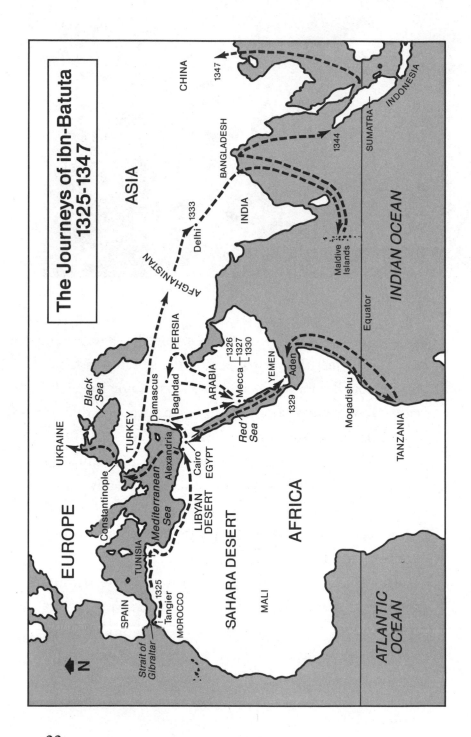

The Journeys of ibn-Batuta
1325-1347

EUROPE

SPAIN

TUNISIA

Strait of
Gibraltar

Tangier
MOROCCO
1325

Mediterranean
Sea

Constantinople

UKRAINE

Black
Sea

TURKEY

Damascus

Alexandria
Cairo
EGYPT

LIBYAN
DESERT

SAHARA DESERT

MALI

AFRICA

ATLANTIC
OCEAN

Red
Sea

Baghdad

PERSIA

ARABIA
Mecca
1326
1327
1330

YEMEN

Aden
1329

Mogadishu

TANZANIA

Equator

INDIAN OCEAN

AFGHANISTAN

Delhi 1333

INDIA

BANGLADESH

Maldive
Islands

1344

SUMATRA

INDONESIA

CHINA

1347

ASIA

N

22

When the sultan asked ibn-Batuta to go to China and give his greetings to the Chinese emperor, the traveler was glad to do so.

This was the unluckiest trip of ibn-Batuta's life. On the way to the coast, where his party was to set sail for China, he was attacked by Hindu rebels. Ibn-Batuta was captured, but escaped after almost being killed. Then, after nearly everyone in the party, except ibn-Batuta and a few others, had boarded the ships, a storm wrecked the fleet and all the ships were lost—along with all the precious gifts ibn-Batuta was supposed to give to the Chinese emperor. Ibn-Batuta was sure of one thing: he did not want to go back to Delhi with this news.

Instead, he set sail for the Maldive Islands, which lie in the Arabian Sea 400 miles southwest of India. There, he made friends with the local ruler and again became a judge. This time, however, he stayed in one place for less than a year.

Between 1344 and 1347, ibn-Batuta traveled east of India, to what is now the country of Bangladesh and to the island of Sumatra in Indonesia. Finally, he reached China. We don't know how far he really got into China, but one thing is sure—he traveled far enough to realize that he had passed the limits of the world he knew. China was as strange a land as any he had seen. He wrote later about odd Chinese things like paper money and about how surprised he was that the roads were safe from robbers. But he did not feel at ease in this beautiful land. Here, the only other Moslems he met were traders in the port cities. He had finally gone beyond the Moslem world.

The time had come to return home. Between the years 1347 and 1349, ibn-Batuta made his way west, passing through India, Persia, Syria, and Arabia, where he made the hajj to Mecca once again. From there, he traveled to Egypt, where he began the last part of his trip, by ship along the coast of North Africa. Near the end of 1349, he arrived home in Tangier. He had been 21 when he left. Now he was 45. His mother and father, he learned, were dead.

Ibn-Batuta took only two more trips. One was to southern Spain, where Moslem rulers were still in power. The other was longer and more dangerous, taking him south across the Sahara Desert to the African kingdom of Mali. When he returned from that final trip, in 1354, the sultan of Morocco asked him to write the story of his travels. This he did, with the help of a younger man. And then ibn-Batuta settled into a quiet life as a lawyer or a judge. In the 15 years he had left to live, he may have wondered how many people knew about his stories and believed them. How surprised ibn-Batuta would be to learn that those stories are still being read more than 600 years later!

2
Vasco da Gama

*F*ive centuries ago, no one knew if it was possible to sail around Africa. Perhaps it would be better to say that people had forgotten. The famous ancient Greek historian Herodotus tells us that sailors from Egypt and Phoenicia made the trip about 2,600 years ago. According to Herodotus, these sailors went from east to west. They started in the Red Sea, circled the huge continent of Africa, and came home by way of the Mediterranean Sea.

In the 1400s, though, the seafaring people of western Europe either had lost track of this story, or thought it was only a legend. They weren't at all sure that they could sail from the Atlantic into the Indian Ocean. Perhaps, they thought, Africa was connected at its southern end to another vast continent, and the Indian Ocean was a sea surrounded by land.

Like many European explorers, the Portuguese mariner Vasco da Gama set sail to gain wealth and power for himself and his country.

For the Europeans, and especially the Portuguese, finding out if a voyage around Africa could really be made was important. Far from Europe, East Asia produced spices, silks, and other fine goods. Two ways had always existed to get these things from Asia to Europe: One way was to carry them over land, in caravans that traveled thousands of miles. The other way was by sea. Arab traders sailed back and forth across the Indian Ocean, bringing goods to the Middle East. From there, caravans would take them by land to the Mediterranean ports used by European merchants.

Both of these routes were problematic. The land route was not only long, but dangerous. If there was trouble among the peoples of central Asia, the trip could not be made at all. And the sea route was expensive. The Europeans had to pay very high prices to the Arabs who had brought the silks and spices from India, China, and the islands of the East Indies.

If the Europeans could discover a sea route around Africa they could overcome both these problems and could control their own trade with the East. This would be especially worthwhile for Portugal, the farthest west of all European countries. Portugal, a poor country, was farthest from the old supply routes. But it was close to Africa's Atlantic coast, and was in a good position to start exploring to the south.

Portugal worked at its chosen task of rounding Africa for nearly a century, taking longer and longer steps along the African coast with each new voyage. During the early years of its African explorations, this small European country was lucky to have a leader whose main interests were seafaring and the distance his captains could carry the Portuguese flag. He was not the king, but one of the king's sons, Prince Henry. For much of his life, Henry lived in a town at the southwestern tip of Portugal, and there he gathered many of his country's bravest sailors. Listening carefully to their reports after each of their voyages, he urged them to press on.

Slowly, the Portuguese solved the African mystery. By 1434, they had accomplished the first step in the journey around Africa. A captain named Gil Eannes became the first Portuguese to sail past Cape Bojador, in West Africa. This was important because of the terrible things people had believed about the sea beyond the cape. Europeans and Arabs had told stories of the "Green Sea of Darkness" that lay beyond this point. This was supposed to be a place where ships would get stuck in thick slime

Henry the Navigator (1394-1460), son of King John I of Portugal, established a school where sailors studied geography and navigation. There, Henry sought to train men who would spread the Christian faith and expand Portuguese trade with Africa and Asia.

and where the sun baked men to a crisp. And, of course, monsters made their dwelling place there.

It was hot, but not so hot that Prince Henry's men couldn't come back to tell where they had been. The Portuguese discovered the mouths of great rivers—the Senegal, the Gambia, the Niger—and coasts where Portugal could buy gold and ivory. Sadly, they also brought back slaves. (The slave trade was a custom of the times, practiced by Europeans, Arabs, and Africans.)

Prince Henry died in 1460, but his captains pushed on. About 1474, Portuguese ships reached the equator. Another 14 years and many more voyages brought the Portuguese close to their dream. Finally, in 1488 all the work brought a great reward. Bartholomew Dias reached the Cape of Good Hope, the southern tip of Africa. A way around the continent from the Atlantic to the Indian Ocean did exist!

Now came the hard part. Looking beyond Africa into the Indian Ocean was one thing, but sailing out into that ocean with any hope of reaching India was quite another. Nearly ten years passed before Portugal was ready to try. During that time, an Italian named Christopher Columbus sailed in a different direction to reach the rich countries of the East. He failed, and no one yet knew that the land he claimed for Spain was not the East Indies. The Portuguese had to make their move, before they were beaten by their Spanish rivals.

In 1497, Portugal fitted four new ships for the voyage

from its capital, Lisbon, around Africa to India. The man chosen to command the fleet was a 27-year-old captain named Vasco da Gama. We know very little about his life before the voyage that would make him famous, except that he was part English and had spent more of his youth as a soldier than as a sailor. We can be sure, however, that he must have been a good sailor, since he was trusted by the king with the most dangerous and important voyage in Portugal's history.

Da Gama's ships left Lisbon on July 8, 1497. On the ships were 170 sailors, hungry for adventure. Unlike many of the explorers of the African coast who had gone before him, da Gama sailed well out into the Atlantic because by that time sailors knew that this was the best way to pick up winds that would carry the sailing ships south to the Cape of Good Hope. When da Gama did reach the Cape, he and his crewmen had been at sea for 13 weeks. No European sailors had ever been out of sight of land as long as they had.

Once they rounded the Cape of Good Hope, the Portuguese sailed along a coast totally unknown to Europeans. No Arabs had ever sailed that far south on Africa's Indian Ocean coast either. Perhaps no one, since that long-ago voyage described by Herodotus, had ever sailed these waters. According to plan, the three largest ships took on all the supplies of the fourth and left it, the smallest, behind. Because the time of the year was the Christmas season, da Gama gave the strange coast the name "Natal," which is the Portuguese word for Christmas. The name survives today, as part of the country of South Africa.

Slowly, after fighting the swift ocean currents that run between Africa and the big island of Madagascar, the three Portuguese ships reached the known world once again. Danger lurked there, however, because the people living on the coast did not welcome Europeans. Moslems ruled the outposts of east Africa, and they were not happy to see European traders. At Mombasa, in the country now called Kenya, da Gama's men had to use cannons to fight off an attack.

Malindi, farther north, was a friendlier port. Here da Gama had his best luck of the voyage. He found an Arab navigator who was willing to guide the ships across the Indian Ocean. Without his help, the Portuguese might never have determined the best way to sail with the ocean's winds. Or, they might not have been able to take their ships safely through the reefs and shallows near the Indian coast.

The three Portuguese ships reached India in late May 1498, more than ten months after they had left Lisbon. They were not given much of a welcome. Arabs managed trade at the ports, and the people of India were happy to leave things that way. Da Gama was able, however, to buy some pepper and cinnamon—two spices that Europeans valued—so at least he would not be going home empty-handed. But he would have to tell

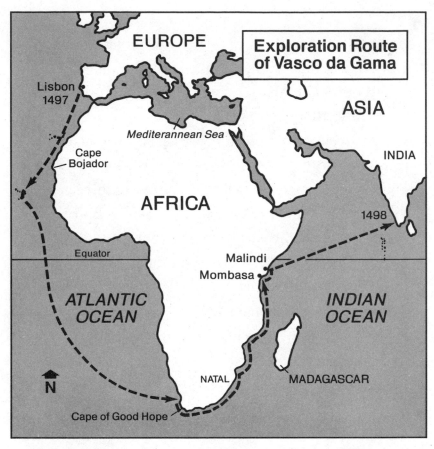

Exploration Route of Vasco da Gama

the king that trading in the East would take more work than just sailing around Africa.

Da Gama almost never got to tell the king anything. The trip back across the Indian Ocean was a terrible one, with fierce storms that damaged one ship so badly that they abandoned it. The two ships that were left would have been jam-packed with 170 men, but nowhere near that many were left as the voyage neared its end. In fact, only 55 sailors returned to Lisbon. The rest, including da Gama's brother, Paulo, had died of illness along the way.

The two remaining ships reached Lisbon in September 1499. They had finished the longest voyage ever made to that time. Portugal greeted da Gama as a great hero. He had finally ended the country's long search for a sea route to the East! As he had learned, though, Portugal would have to fight to win trading rights in India and to take the business of trade away from the Arabs on the Indian Ocean. The little European country did not wait long to begin. Da Gama himself went back to India in 1502, but the main work of conquest was done by an admiral who was a genius, Alfonso de Alboquerque. In only three years, beginning in 1509, Alboquerque took all the important Indian Ocean trading stations from the Arabs, conquered the west coast of India, and cleared the way for Portuguese ships to sail as far as China and the Spice Islands.

Vasco da Gama went to India for the last time in 1524. While serving as royal governor, he died there in that year. But he had lived to see a new Portuguese empire, and he knew that he was one of the men who had made this possible. This empire was not to be one of history's longer-lasting, however. In fact, if da Gama had come back 100 years later, he would have seen Portugal's far eastern trade being taken over by the Dutch and the English, just as the Portuguese had taken it from the Arabs. But no one could take from Portugal the glory of being the first European nation to brave the "Green Sea of Darkness" and find a way around Africa.

As an island nation, England attached great importance to mastery of the seas. The English reserved deep admiration for their country's seafaring heroes, including Captain James Cook.

3

James Cook

Just over 200 years ago, the Pacific Ocean was a great blank space on the map. Along the western shores of the Pacific lived the Chinese, Japanese, and the islanders of the East Indies, but none of these peoples had ever sailed far upon the Pacific, the largest of the world's oceans. Europeans had known about the Pacific since 1513, when the Spanish explorer Vasco de Balboa first saw it. Spanish and English captains had crossed the Pacific while sailing around the world, and Spanish ships made the long cross-Pacific trip each year carrying goods between Mexico and the Philippine Islands. But no one had ever tried to explore the Pacific carefully. No one from Europe had tried to map its hundreds and hundreds of islands.

Only six years after Vasco de Balboa (1475-1519) claimed the Pacific Ocean and the lands it touched for his native Spain, the Spanish government accused him of treason and beheaded him.

Into this vast, largely uncharted ocean, in the year 1769, came the greatest sea explorer who ever lived. His name was Captain James Cook, and he had been sent from England to learn as much as he could about the Pacific and its islands.

James Cook was born in 1728, in a part of England called Yorkshire. His father worked on another man's farm. That was not the sort of job young James wanted for himself, so at the age of 17 he left home for a town on the seacoast. There, a year later, he got his first chance to work on a ship.

For the next nine years, James Cook sailed on ships that carried coal up and down the English coast and to places as far away as Norway. Between voyages, he stayed up late each night studying to become a better sailor. He taught himself the hard subject of navigation, the science of finding one's way in a ship at sea. In Cook's time, ships had no computers or radar. A captain had to tell where he was by watching the sun and the stars in the sky, and he needed to know mathematics well.

By the time he was 27, James Cook was such a good sailor that a coal ship owner asked him to become a captain. He was very young for such an important job, and he must have been proud to have been chosen. But Cook turned down the offer. Instead of carrying coal from one port to another, he wanted a more exciting job. So, he joined the British Navy.

Like all other ships in those days, "men o'war"—the name given to the fighting ships—were made of wood and powered by the wind. Sailing them was hard, dangerous work, even when the ships were not in battle. Crews were large, and only the finest men could lead them well. Obviously, the captains for whom James Cook worked could see that he was such a man because in only two years he was promoted to ship's master. Next to the captain and other officers, this was the highest rank on a ship. Soon after Cook joined, Britain went to war with France. This war decided which country would control Canada. Britain needed a map of the St. Lawrence River so that its ships could safely travel up river when they attacked Quebec, the French capital. They sent Cook's ship across the Atlantic to Canada to map the river. Cook did his work so well that after Britain won the war, they asked him to make more maps and sea charts of the Canadian coast. He worked at this task, off and on, for the next nine years.

James Cook was almost 40 years old when he had finished his work in Canada. He had married and become a father, but like most sailors he was often away from his family for many months or even years. We know little about Cook's wife and children, for he seldom wrote about personal things. What we do know is that by the time he returned from Canada, he was known as one of the best chart-makers and wisest masters in the British Navy.

Because of Cook's skills as a chart-maker, leader of men, and navigator, the navy gave him the command to explore. A group of scientists called the Royal Society had asked the navy to send a ship to the Pacific Ocean to find new islands and to map others that were already known. The scientists had another reason for asking the navy to explore the Pacific. They wondered if there really was a great continent south of the Atlantic and Pacific oceans, as some people believed. Everyone agreed that the best leader for this voyage would be James Cook. Thus, he became Lieutenant James Cook, an officer of the British Navy.

Cook and a crew of 93, including scientists and sailors, left England in the ship *Endeavor* in August 1768. *Endeavor* was a coal ship. They chose this ship not because of Cook's old job, but because coal ships were big and wide, held a lot of cargo, and could sail well—but not fast—in all kinds of weather.

Cook needed a ship with plenty of room that could carry food and supplies for two years or more. He made sure to stock sauerkraut, along with fruits and vegetables that would keep a long time. In those days, many sailors died from a disease called scurvy, and smart captains had learned that these kinds of foods kept sailors healthy. We know now that these foods are rich in vitamin C.

Cook cared so much about the health of his men that he even had two sailors whipped because they would not eat the right foods. Whipping, called flogging, was a common punishment 200 years ago. But Cook was not a cruel man. His men, even those whom he had punished, always loved him.

Endeavor sailed across the Atlantic Ocean to South America, stopping in Brazil for food and fresh water. Then came the first really hard part of the trip: sailing through the dangerous waters around Cape Horn, at the southern-most tip of South America. (Our modern shortcut, the Panama Canal, was not built for another 140 years.)

Endeavor rounded Cape Horn and reached the Pacific Ocean in late January 1769. Cook steered his ship far out into the Pacific, towards the island of Tahiti, where only two European ships had ever been before. The vist to Tahiti was important, because the scientists on *Endeavor* had brought a special instrument called a *quadrant* to observe the planet Venus as it passed between the earth and the sun on June 3, 1769. In fact, that was one of the reasons for the trip, since Tahiti was one of the few places on earth where they could watch this event. They almost did not get to watch the eclipse because several of the Tahiti natives stole the shiny quadrant, not knowing what it was! But Cook and his men got it back in time. Afterward the Tahitians and the English got along fairly well.

The beauty of these South Sea islands dazzled the English sailors. To this day, the islands are among the most lovely places on earth, and they must have looked especially fine to men who had been cooped up on a ship for eight months. When, after three months, *Endeavor* sailed from Tahiti, the men were sad to leave. But their leader had more exploring to do. Would he find the unknown continent?

We know now that the ice-covered continent of Antarctica lies at the bottom of the globe, but the men of the Royal Society were hoping to find something much larger—a warm continent where people could live. But there was no such place. After visiting another

From the bow of the Endeavor, *James Cook sights the coast of New Zealand, whose islands he would chart for the first time.*

group of islands, Cook sailed *Endeavor* 1,500 miles south and found only open sea. So he went west, to a place called New Zealand, which no European had seen since Abel Janszoon Tasman, a Dutch explorer, sighted it 126 years earlier.

On this voyage, Cook discovered that New Zealand is made up of two islands. He found the route between them, which is called Cook Strait to this day. While exploring New Zealand, the English sailors fought several battles with the local people, the Maoris. At more peaceful landing places, *Endeavor*'s scientists collected birds and plants and drew pictures of the new kinds of animals and trees they saw.

Next, Cook sailed along the east coast of Australia, the great island-continent that had been sighted years before, but never explored. As always, Cook carefully charted the coast and named each feature of land as he went along. (Many of these names are still in use.) At one point, *Endeavor* ran against the hard coral of the Great Barrier Reef and was badly damaged. When Cook's men ran the ship ashore to repair it, they saw their first kangaroos. They also met the Australian aborigines, a shy people who did not welcome them, as the Tahitians had done, or fight them, as had the Maoris of New Zealand.

Endeavor had now sailed halfway around the world, and the time had come to turn homeward. The route Cook chose took him and his men west between Australia and New Guinea, then to the East Indies, where they were able to stop for supplies at the Dutch settlement on the island of Java. This was an unlucky stop. Many of the sailors, who had been healthy since leaving England, became sick here with dysentery, an infection that causes pain, fever, and severe diarrhea. Some of Cook's men died, including the young artist, Sydney Parkinson, who had made 1,500 drawings of the plants and animals discovered during the trip.

With his crew weak from sickness, Cook had to hire new sailors when *Endeavor* stopped at Cape Town,

James Cook at the Cape of Good Hope, as he appeared to the ship's artist, John Webber (1750-1793)

South Africa. From there, the journey home took three months. *Endeavor* finally reached England on July 12, 1771, nearly three years after it had set sail.

Just one year later, Cook, with his new rank of commander, took to sea again. This time, they gave him two ships, *Resolution* and *Adventure*, and told him to go wherever he wished in the Pacific. Again he brought scientists with him, and again he looked for the southern continent. Far to the south of Africa, he became the first man to sail a ship across the Antarctic Circle.

After making his way across the loneliest part of the Indian Ocean, Cook once again reached New Zealand—the first land he and his men had seen for

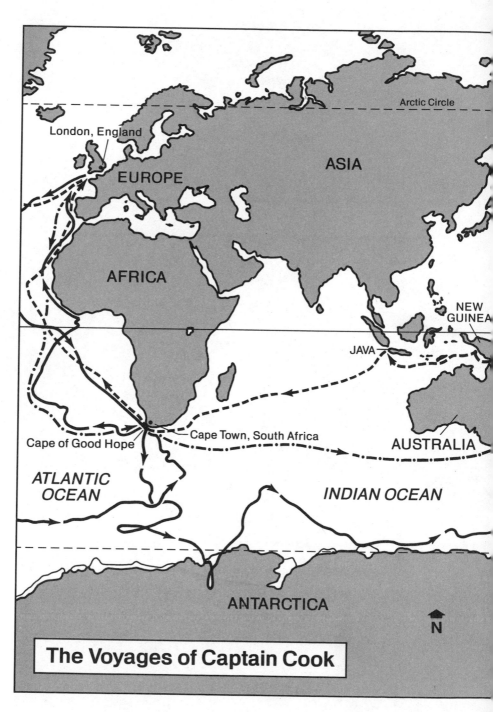

The Voyages of Captain Cook

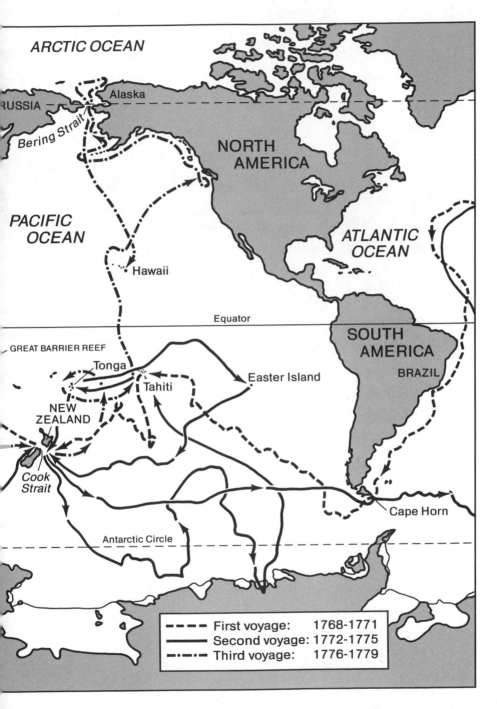

ARCTIC OCEAN

RUSSIA

Alaska

Bering Strait

NORTH
AMERICA

PACIFIC
OCEAN

ATLANTIC
OCEAN

Hawaii

Equator

SOUTH
AMERICA

GREAT BARRIER REEF

BRAZIL

Tonga

Easter Island

Tahiti

NEW
ZEALAND

Cook
Strait

Cape Horn

Antarctic Circle

	First voyage:	1768-1771
	Second voyage:	1772-1775
	Third voyage:	1776-1779

45

four months. But instead of sailing from New Zealand into warmer waters, Cook took *Resolution* south. *Adventure* had gone back to England after the Maoris killed some of her crew. This time, *Resolution* sailed as far south as Cook would ever go. He would have discovered the continent of Antarctica, had he not run into a sea of solid ice.

What did Cook's men think of him? We can tell by their answer when he asked them now if they wanted to go home, or if they wanted to explore for another year. They voted to keep sailing, even though they were almost worn out from working with frozen ropes and sails.

Resolution next visited familiar places—the islands of Tahiti and Tonga. Then, before returning to New Zealand and getting ready for the trip home, Cook took his ship to one of the strangest places in the Pacific— Easter Island. Here the sailors marveled at the huge stone heads set into the island's hillsides. Who carved these heads? We know little more about them now than people did in Cook's day.

Resolution returned home by heading east around South America and crossing the South Atlantic for one last look for the continent that wasn't there. The ship arrived in England in July 1775, three years after it had set sail. When they arrived, Cook and his men might have heard the news that the American Revolution had begun while they were at sea.

Cook returned a great hero, and they finally gave

him the rank of captain. For a while he stayed in England, with plenty of time to talk and write about his travels. But when he heard of plans for another Pacific exploration, Captain Cook wanted to be in charge.

This time, the captain's task would be to look for the Northwest Passage, the name people gave to a route through the Arctic Ocean, around the top of North America. We know now that this route is too dangerous to use, because it is choked with ice nearly all year round. But Captain Cook was asked to find it and to follow it from the Pacific to the Atlantic Ocean.

Again Cook captained the *Resolution*: another ship, named *Discovery*, sailed with him. The ships left England in the summer of 1776 and spent a good part of the next year at the familiar islands of Tonga and Tahiti. Captain Cook was not supposed to try to sail the Northwest Passage until the summer of 1778, when a ship coming from the Atlantic Ocean was to meet him there. During this waiting time, Cook made one important discovery— a group of islands called Hawaii. Cook named them the Sandwich Islands, after his friend, Lord Sandwich.

When the time came to try the Northwest Passage, Cook took *Resolution* up along the coast of North America, then west around Alaska and through the Bering Strait that separates Alaska from Russia. But here he had the same problem he had had at the southern end of the earth: ice blocked his way. So he headed south, back to Hawaii, and planned to try again the next year.

But there would be no next year for Captain Cook. In February of 1779, when Hawaiian natives stole one of *Discovery*'s small boats, Cook tried to take their king prisoner until the natives returned the boat. A fight started, and Cook was killed.

When *Resolution* and *Discovery* finally reached home with the news of their captain's death, all of England mourned. Artists made statues and monuments to honor the great explorer. But the best monuments to Captain Cook are his excellent maps. These show a part of the world that was hardly known when he began sailing. Further honors to him are the hundreds of names he gave to the places he discovered. Even today, we cannot travel in the Pacific without being reminded of James Cook, a Yorkshire boy who went to sea.

Captain Cook left detailed maps that helped travelers to find their way many years after his death.

The early seventeenth-century Frenchman, Samuel de Champlain, explored most of Canada's eastern provinces, including Nova Scotia, New Brunswick, Quebec, and Ontario.

4
Samuel de Champlain

*O*ne warm afternoon in August 1867, a 14-year-old boy was helping his father clear trees from a patch of land near the town of Cobden, in Canada's Ottawa valley. He had hitched a team of oxen to a heavy log that was lying on the ground and, when the log broke loose, the boy saw a metal object sticking out of the mossy soil.

Little did the boy know, as he handed the odd circle to his father, that he had found a wonderful relic of the early age of Canadian exploration. The object was an astrolabe. This device, used for reading the position of the sun, helped tell travelers their position on the earth's surface. The instrument had been lost in 1613, by none other than Samuel de Champlain.

Samuel de Champlain was the greatest figure in the history of New France, the French colony in America, and he may fairly be called the "Father of Canada." His explorations took him along the Atlantic coast from Nova Scotia to Cape Cod, Massachusetts, and from the mouth of the St. Lawrence River to Lake Huron, deep in the Canadian interior. He was the discoverer of the lake that lies between New York state and Vermont. This beautiful lake still bears his name. He was the founder of Quebec, the oldest city north of Florida on the North American continent. And when his years of discovery were over, he served New France wisely as its governor.

Champlain was born about 1567—historians are not quite sure about the date—in the French seacoast town of Brouage. His father was a fishing-boat captain. Although he learned seamanship as a boy, Champlain spent much of his time as a young man in the French Army, fighting on the side of King Henry IV against rebels in the province of Brittany.

When he left the army in 1598, the 31-year-old Champlain was ready to seek new adventures. First he went to Spain, where he had an uncle who got him a place on a ship headed for the Spanish colonies in the New World. He visited the Caribbean islands of Guadeloupe, Puerto Rico, and Hispaniola and then sailed on to Cuba and Mexico. Reaching Panama, he wondered whether a canal might be cut across this narrow place between the Atlantic and the Pacific oceans—as indeed one was, more than 300 years later. Champlain may even have visited Florida. All along the way, he kept notes, made maps, and drew beautiful pictures of the strange birds, animals, fish, and plants he had seen. When he got back to France in 1601, he put all his material together into a handwritten book.

After the voyage to the Caribbean, Samuel de Champlain was sure about what he wanted to do with his life. Now that he had seen how Spain had taken its share of the riches of the Americas, he thought that his country, France, might also find new greatness across the sea. So, in March of 1603, Champlain joined a trading voyage to the St. Lawrence River in Canada.

This was not the beginning of France's interest in Canada. In 1534 and 1535, and again in 1541, Jacques Cartier had explored Canada's Atlantic coast and had carried the French flag far up the St. Lawrence River to where the city of Montreal now stands. Other French explorers had followed him. But when Champlain first sailed for Canada, a few hardy fur-traders were the only Frenchmen actually living in this vast land. There were no real towns, only a trading post at the point where the Saguenay River flows into the St. Lawrence.

This trading post, called Tadoussac, was Champlain's first landing place in Canada. Here he first met the Algonquin Indians who were to be his allies in later years. He listened to the Indians' stories of the

In 1535, French explorer Jacques Cartier (1491-1557) met with Indians in their village—Hochelaga—which a century later would be called the city of Montreal.

places that lay beyond the St. Lawrence valley—the Hudson River, the Great Lakes, Niagara Falls, and Hudson Bay. No white men had yet visited these places. During his stay of only three months, Champlain could not hope to venture far into the vast continent. But he listened carefully, took notes, and even explored up river as far as the wild rapids near the site where, 39 years later, his countrymen would establish the city of Montreal.

When he returned to France in the fall of 1603, Champlain again put all he had learned into a book. This time, many copies were printed. When a new expedition to Canada prepared to set out in the spring of 1604, the government asked him to go along as the official mapmaker.

This time, the plan of the voyage was not only to sail down the St. Lawrence, but also to scout along the Atlantic coast for possible settlement sites. The expedition leader, Sieur (Sir) de Monts, took his ship around the western tip of Nova Scotia and entered the Bay of Fundy, which separates Nova Scotia from Maine. (None of these names, of course, had yet been given. The French simply called the region "Acadia.")

After spending the rest of the summer and early fall exploring the river mouths of Maine and the future Canadian province of New Brunswick, de Monts and his men built winter shelters on an island in Passamaquoddy Bay, where the Canada-United States border now begins. A terrible time lay ahead. Before spring arrived, 35 of the 79 French crewmen died from scurvy, a disease caused by lack of vitamin C. Snow covered the ground well into May. Finally in June, when de Monts, Champlain, and the other survivors had nearly lost hope, a ship from France reached their island with food and supplies. Now a new season of exploration could begin.

During the warm months of 1605, and again in 1606, Champlain had many chances to use his map-making skills as his party explored the coast of New England as far south as Cape Cod. They became the first Europeans to visit the site that later became known as Boston, and they even sailed into the bay where the English Pilgrims would land 15 years later. They landed often to see if the soil was good for farming, and in many places, they met the local Indian tribes. Only twice did trouble occur. Indian arrows killed one French sailor on Cape Cod in 1605, and four more sailors died during a disagreement near the same place in 1606. These two incidents were enough to keep the French from exploring so far south in following years. They decided to begin their settlements in Acadia and along the St. Lawrence valley. New France would stay where it was, and New England would be left to become . . . New England.

The French explorers spent the winters of 1605 and 1606 at a much better place than the barren island in Passamaquoddy Bay. They found a beautiful spot on a hill above an inlet of the Bay of Fundy, in Nova Scotia, and built a snug fort which they called Port-Royal. The local Indians were helpful, and more settlers from France arrived to join the group. Champlain, as the mapmaker, was not in charge of the settlement, but he was one of the leading men, and he came up with a fine idea to make the long winters pass more quickly. He called his idea the "Order of Good Cheer." Champlain suggested that the men make a contest of hunting, so that there would be plenty of meat on the table during winter. Each night became a feast, as if the settlers were in a jolly club in Paris instead of in the wilderness. (The Canadian government has built a copy of the wooden Port-Royal buildings on the exact spot where they stood. A visitor to Nova Scotia, can walk through rooms just like those Champlain and his companions lived in and imagine the songs and laughter of the "Order.")

The Frenchmen left Port-Royal in August 1607. They arrived in France one month later. Back home again, Champlain reported that the St. Lawrence valley, after all, would be the best place to build more trading posts and to bring French settlers. The king of France agreed, and Champlain was put in charge of a new expedition up the great river.

Champlain sailed for Canada in April 1608.

Like many of the Europeans who first traveled to North America, Champlain traded jewelry and tools, such as axes and knives, for the Indians' furs.

Stopping at Tadoussac only long enough to gather supplies, he continued up the St. Lawrence until he reached a mighty cliff that juts into the river. Here, on July 3, he planted the French flag and founded the town of Quebec. There the city stands today, capital of the province of Quebec.

Champlain spent the following year organizing a fur-trading post at Quebec. He had to deal with a bad winter and the mutiny of some of his men. But by late spring 1609, he was ready to go exploring once again. He chose to head farther up the St. Lawrence, then south. He took with him a number of the Algonquin Indians who had made friends with the French at Quebec and who were old enemies of the Iroquois who lived farther south. Champlain and his Indian allies were looking for the Iroquois, which surely meant they were looking for trouble.

Traveling up the St. Lawrence to the Richelieu River, then south along the Richelieu, Champlain came to a great lake between two mountain ranges. He named this "Lake Champlain." Standing by the lake, Champlain was the first European to look upon the Adirondacks of New York and the Green Mountains of Vermont.

As they paddled south on the lake, the Algonquins knew they were heading deeper into the land of their enemies. Finally the moment came: the French-Indian party reached an Iroquois camp. When Champlain

Champlain and his Algonquin allies skirmish with fierce Iroquois Indians. Iroquois arrows, however, were no match for the French firearms.

thought that he had sighted some of the Iroquois reaching for their bows, he fired his musket and killed two chiefs.

The Iroquois fled, and the power of their French allies thrilled the Algonquins. But without knowing it, Champlain had started 150 years of war between the French and the Iroquois. By taking sides, he kept his allies. But he had made an enemy that would one day help the English take Canada from the French.

During the next few years, Champlain traveled back and forth several times between Canada and France. He was eager to keep the king interested in the faraway French colony, which had not yet made anyone much money. By now, Champlain had a greater idea of what New France could be. He did not want it to remain just a string of tiny posts where men traded with the Indians for furs. He wanted a real colony, with hundreds of settlers coming from France to farm, to build towns, and to raise families. This was what New France would one day become—largely because of the man whose statue stands today overlooking the St. Lawrence River in the busy city of Quebec.

But even though he was now in his forties, Champlain wanted to keep busy exploring as well as talking and writing. Could he find his way to the Great Lakes or to Hudson Bay, which he had heard the Indians tell of during his first trip to Canada?

In 1613, Champlain set out for the West. By canoe, he and his party ventured beyond the future site of Montreal and headed up the Ottawa River. Champlain was hoping that this river would take him to a great inland sea, perhaps Hudson Bay. But it was not to be. The Ottawa goes nowhere near Hudson Bay, and the young woodsman, who had told Champlain it did, admitted he had lied.

Somewhere along the way down the Ottawa, Champlain must have realized that he had forgotten something at the last stopping place. His astrolabe! No doubt he decided that heading back to look for it was not worth the effort. Or, if he did return, he was unable to find the missing item. Did he wonder if it would ever be found?

The year 1615 brought one last try on the part of Champlain to learn the secrets of the rivers and lakes to the west. This time, the nearly 50-year-old Champlain led his party far past his 1613 turnaround point, to a series of lakes and rivers in what is now the Canadian province of Ontario. Along the way, the party of explorers crossed Lake Nipissing, where the eastern Algonquin Indians had told them they would meet a tribe of evil sorcerers. But the Nipissings gave the Frenchmen a friendly greeting and allowed them to head even farther west, to a much greater body of water. Would this be the inland arm of the ocean Champlain was searching for?

Georgian Bay is a part of Lake Huron, one of the Great Lakes. For anyone approaching it from the east, as Champlain did, the western shore cannot be seen. We can picture Champlain cupping his hand into the water, and frowning in disappointment when he tasted no ocean salt. Hudson Bay was 400 miles to the north, and the Pacific Ocean 2,000 miles farther west!

Champlain turned his canoes south along Georgian Bay and headed east through the lakes and rivers of the Huron Indian country. His party reached the eastern end of Lake Ontario and finally saw where the St. Lawrence—the river highway of New France—had its source.

Then Champlain faced the Iroquois once again. The Hurons, too, were enemies of the Iroquois, and they

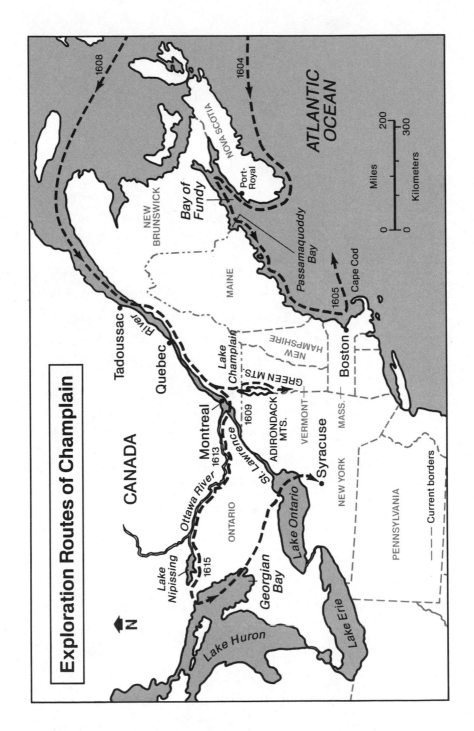

Exploration Routes of Champlain

CANADA

ATLANTIC OCEAN

NOVA SCOTIA

NEW BRUNSWICK

Bay of Fundy

Port-Royal

Passamaquoddy Bay

Cape Cod

MAINE

NEW HAMPSHIRE

Boston

Tadoussac

Quebec

River

Lake Champlain

GREEN MTS.

ADIRONDACK MTS.

VERMONT

MASS.

Montreal

St. Lawrence

Syracuse

NEW YORK

Ottawa River

ONTARIO

PENNSYLVANIA

Lake Nipissing

Lake Ontario

Georgian Bay

Lake Erie

Lake Huron

1608

1604

1605

1609

1613

1615

200

300

Miles

Kilometers

Current borders

N

urged their French friends to attack an Iroquois fort near the spot where Syracuse, New York, now stands. This time, however, the French and their allies lost. Two arrows wounded Champlain. When he and the Indians reached Lake Ontario, Champlain wanted to head straight down the St. Lawrence to Quebec, but the Hurons refused. They wanted to go home their way, which meant a long, roundabout trip for the wounded man through Georgian Bay and along the Ottawa River. Only in July 1616, did Champlain see Quebec again.

Samuel de Champlain had nearly 20 years of life left to him when this last great exploration was over. He spent it as before, sailing back and forth between New and Old France, meanwhile working on a book about his adventures and the history of the colony. Then, while he was at Quebec in 1629, he saw his life's work nearly undone. England had been at war with France, and an English fleet sailed up the St. Lawrence to capture the French colony. Champlain surrendered and the commander of the fleet took him to England as a prisoner. But on arriving, the English commander learned that the war was over, and France was to keep Quebec after all.

Champlain finally returned to Quebec in 1633. He spent two years governing the colony, even though he was never officially made governor, and died at Quebec in 1635. During these last years, he did his best to keep the Algonquins and Hurons as allies, since he knew the

Champlain and his men build a wall on the site that would become Montreal, which today is the second largest French-speaking city in the world.

Iroquois would always be a threat. But his great work of keeping France interested in its colony had been done. New France would grow, and even after England took over, in 1763, French ways and the French language would survive in Canada. They survive still, in La Belle Province, "the beautiful province" of Quebec.

5
Jacques Marquette

*T*he greatest river in North America remained a mystery to Europeans for many years after they began to penetrate the continent. The early Spanish explorers knew that a huge river emptied into the Gulf of Mexico, and a Spaniard named Hernando de Soto visited the southern parts of the river in 1541. But no one knew how far north the river began. The source of the mighty Mississippi lay deep within the continent, in lands that had yet to be explored by Europeans.

The man who finally reached the upper Mississippi was not a soldier, like de Soto, or a fur-trader like many of the other men who explored North America. He was Jacques Marquette, called Père Marquette because he was a Catholic priest. ("Père" means "father" in French). Père Marquette was one of the brave members

Through his explorations, Jacques Marquette sought to spread the Catholic faith rather than gain personal wealth.

of the Jesuit order of priests who came to French Canada in its earliest days to teach the Catholic religion to the Indians. Like many Jesuits, his travels among the Indians brought him so deep into unknown territory that he deserves the title of explorer.

Jacques Marquette was born in the French city of Laon, in the year 1637. He was the son of one of the city's most famous families, and his father was a friend of the French king. Young Jacques probably could have grown up to be a rich and important man in Laon, but he was mostly interested in studying and in religion. He attended Jesuit schools and, when he was only 17, he began the 12 long years of study that would make him a Jesuit priest.

During the years he was at school, Jacques Marquette surely read of the danger-filled lives of other brave French Jesuits who were working in the wilderness of faraway Quebec. Each year, the priests in Quebec sent home an account of their work among the Indians. This yearly account, called the *Jesuit Relations*, also told everything that was being learned about the vast land that France had claimed along the St. Lawrence River. To a young student like Jacques, the *Relations* must have seemed like a call to special service.

And called he was. In 1666, his Jesuit superiors ordered Père Marquette, who had finished his studies and been made a priest, to go to Quebec and teach the

Based in the Spanish colony of Cuba, Hernando de Soto (1500-1542) explored the southern United States, including Florida, Georgia, Alabama, Mississippi, Tennessee, and Texas. He and his men were probably the first Europeans to cross the Mississippi River.

Indians. He knew that he might never see France again, but he was eager to live the life he had read about in the *Relations*.

Père Marquette landed at Quebec, the fortress town on the St. Lawrence River, in September 1666. Quebec in those days was a long way from being the handsome city it is today. The young priest found a few streets of small houses, a church, a hospital, and the buildings where the priests and nuns lived. The most important places in the town were the governor's house and the storehouse for furs. Quebec, after all, was mainly a fur-trading town.

Marquette saw his first Indians in Quebec. In the years since they had first come to Canada, the French had made friends with some of the Indian tribes that lived along the St. Lawrence valley. Members of the Huron tribes traded furs with the French, and these were among the first Indians to be taught by the French priests. South of Quebec, however, lived Iroquois tribes who were enemies of the French. During the 1600s, the French and Iroquois fought each other many times, and the Iroquois captured and killed several Jesuit priests.

After only three weeks in Quebec, Marquette's superiors ordered him to head east along the St. Lawrence River to the settlement of Trois Rivieres—in English, "Three Rivers." There he would study the local Indian languages and get ready to begin teaching. While he was at Trois Rivieres, he also learned about Indian life and customs from other priests who had been in the wilderness and lived among them.

Once he had been trained and had spent two years teaching in the east, Marquette received orders to head west, deep into the country of the Ottawa Indians. (Ottawa today, is the name of the capital of Canada.) With three helpers, Marquette traveled by canoe up through the valley of the Ottawa River, then through forests and across lakes to Lake Huron. His goal was the northern end of Lake Huron, where there was an Indian village called Sault (pronounced "Soo") Saint Marie. Here, and at other small Indian settlements near the place where the Great Lakes of Huron and Michigan come together, Marquette lived and worked for five years.

A modern map shows that Marquette's territory was in the northern part of the state of Michigan. Indians from farther south and west would sometimes travel to the villages where he taught, and when they did, he often heard them talk of a great river to the west. It flowed south into a warmer land, they said, and its name was "Mississippi."

That such a river might exist excited Marquette. If what the Indians said were true, the river might some-day be a highway for spreading the Catholic faith and the power of France as well. He probably never thought that he would ever find the river. His work was with the Indians in northern Michigan. But back in Quebec, the leaders of French Canada were planning an exploration of the West. They, too, had heard tales of the Mississippi. As head of the exploration party, they chose a young fur-trader named Louis Joliet, who knew Marquette. Someone—perhaps Joliet, or perhaps the Jesuits in Quebec—suggested that Père Marquette go along as the expedition's priest.

In December 1672, Marquette was living at the Indian village of St. Ignace, on the Straits of Mackinac between Lakes Michigan and Huron. The priest had settled in for the winter with his Indian hosts. Then, on December 8, who should appear but his old friend Joliet, with news of the orders from Quebec! They were to search for the Mississippi, and they were to leave in the spring as soon as the ice melted.

With five men to help paddle their two canoes and carry supplies, Marquette and Joliet left St. Ignace on May 17, 1673. First they followed the north shore of Lake Michigan, slowly turning southwest toward what is now the state of Wisconsin. These must have been fine days of travel. Staying close to the shore, they avoided the rough waters farther out in the lake, and unless a wind was blowing against them, they could paddle along at three or four miles an hour. They slept under the stars at night, and their chief foods were dried meat and Indian cornmeal—until they got further west, where the delicious grain called wild rice grew.

The small party paddled south into Green Bay, along the east shore of Wisconsin, and followed the bay

Fur-trader Louis Joliet (1645-1700) joined Marquette to search for the great Mississippi River, which Europeans had known of only from the Indians' descriptions.

to its end. From here they could head upstream along the Fox River, which flowed through a beautiful country just turning green with spring. Four years before, a French Jesuit had visited a friendly Indian village on the banks of the Fox. Here they found two Indian guides, who traveled along with them and showed them where they could carry their canoes from the Fox to the Wisconsin River. This was an important passage. On the Fox, they paddled in waters that flowed east to the Great Lakes and the St. Lawrence. Once they struggled over high ground and dropped their bark canoes into the Wisconsin River, they were on a waterway that led to the Mississippi.

The Wisconsin is a swift and wild river, especially in springtime when the melted snow of the past winter feeds it. The canoes raced faster and faster with the current, until the Wisconsin lost itself in a far greater river. On June 17, one month after starting out, Marquette and Joliet reached their goal. Except for the Indian guides, who had gone home once the party had reached the Wisconsin River, they had had nothing to go by but a few simple maps they had drawn, based on what the Indians had told them about the rivers west of Lake Michigan. But they had reached the Mississippi. They were the first Europeans to venture upon it this far north.

Having come this far, the Frenchmen's next plan was to paddle as far south as they could on the big river and perhaps to reach the sea. Riding with the current, they began the southward trip. After eight days they reached a village of friendly Illinois Indians, who fed them well and smoked the *calumet*, or peace pipe, with them. The chief gave Marquette a calumet, which he held up and shared as a sign of friendship when the party met other Indians farther to the south.

As the two canoes continued past the points where the Missouri and Ohio rivers flow into the Mississippi, forests gave way to prairies. In the notebook he kept,

During his travels, Marquette used the peace pipe to show the Indians that he posed no threat to them.

Marquette wrote about the strange new things he saw. Perhaps the strangest were the "wild cattle" of the plains, great shaggy beasts with horns and humped backs—the buffalo.

Finally, Marquette and Joliet realized that traveling further south would not be wise. They could tell that this was the same great river that flowed into the Gulf of Mexico. Why risk meeting fierce tribes closer to the coast or perhaps even capture by the Spaniards? So they decided to turn back. They didn't know it, but they had the best of reasons: they were still 700 miles from the Gulf!

The route home took them back against the Mississippi's strong current, but not for as far as they

Marquette and Joliet canoe down the Mississippi River with their Indian guides.

had come downstream. This time, they left the Mississippi at the Illinois River, which they followed north towards Lake Michigan. Along the way, the travelers must have passed not far from where the city of Chicago would be built, almost 200 years later.

Marquette and Joliet soon went their separate ways. The priest, who had been sick, stayed to rest at the little Indian mission on the Fox River near Green Bay, where they had stopped on the way to the Mississippi. Joliet went on to Quebec to report to the governor on the expedition. But Joliet lost the report and the maps he

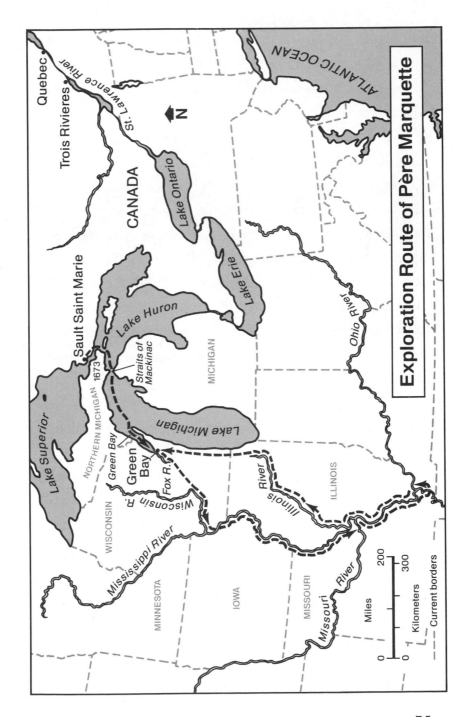

Exploration Route of Père Marquette

had made in a canoe accident near Montreal. What we know of this first European trip to the northern Mississippi comes instead from the notes taken by Marquette.

The Jesuit priest did not take those notes to Quebec himself. After resting in Wisconsin, he was ordered to go south again to work among the Illinois Indians. This was in 1674. Marquette was only 37 years old, but he had never been a strong man, and the journey back to Illinois weakened him further. By April 1675, he was too sick to remain at his post. He left for Quebec by canoe, but had gotten no further than the eastern shore of Lake Michigan when he asked his paddlers to head for land. There he was carried ashore, and there he died and was buried.

Père Marquette probably didn't live as long as he would have had he stayed rich and safe in Laon. But he had done what he felt was his duty—he had won love and respect from the Indians, and he would be remembered as one of the discoverers of the Mississippi River.

This 1910 monument honoring Marquette stands more than 50 feet high and is located in Prairie du Chien, Wisconsin, just three miles north of where the French priest first reached the Mississippi.

Business pursuits took Alexander Mackenzie from eastern Canada to the vast, unexplored West, where he discovered places that no European had seen before.

6
Alexander Mackenzie

*W*hen we talk about the reasons people explore new places, we don't usually think about fads and fashions. But some of the great explorations of North America were made because of hat styles. Much of Canada was explored because people in Europe once had a great liking for hats made of fur felt—felt made from beaver fur.

Canada is a land of great rivers and thousands of lakes. It has been said that one-third of all the fresh water on earth is in Canada. With all that water, Canada is a perfect home for beaver. The early explorers sent the rich beaver fur back to Europe, where it became a popular material for hats.

From the time of the earliest French settlers in eastern Canada, fur-traders pushed farther and farther west into the wilderness. They worked with Canada's Indian tribes, who trapped beaver and sold the furs to the white men in return for blankets and tools. Living among the Indians, the white traders learned the Indian way to travel on Canada's rivers and lakes. They learned that the best way to get around in the backwoods of Canada was by canoe. The Indians' canoes were made of birch bark, which is light and strong. The traders could paddle even in water only a few inches deep and could carry them easily when there was dry land to cross.

As the years went by, the fur-traders paddled their canoes deep into Canada. But none of the rivers and lakes they followed brought them all the way across Canada, to the Pacific Ocean. Could men in canoes make such a trip? In the late 1780s, a young Scot named Alexander Mackenzie decided to find out.

Alexander Mackenzie was born in 1764, on the island of Lewis near Scotland's northwest coast. When Alexander was ten, his mother died, and his father took the boy to New York. But America would not be a peaceful home for the Mackenzies. One year later, the American Revolution began. Alexander's father fought on the side of the English and sent Alexander to live with relatives in the countryside. Later he went to school in Montreal, Canada. This was a safer place for people who were still loyal to England.

Like many boys of his time, Alexander Mackenzie left school early and went to work in the office of a fur-trading company. After he had worked in Montreal for five years, the firm gave him a more important job, at a trading post deep in the Canadian forests.

In 1788, when he was only 24, Mackenzie was put in charge of the farthest of all his company's trading posts. This was a desolate spot on Lake Athabasca, in a far northern corner of the province of Saskatchewan in Canada. The land around Lake Athabasca is still wild today, and few people live there. In Mackenzie's time, the area must have been lonely indeed. The only people he saw were the white fur-traders, who came each summer from the East, and the Indians who brought furs to the post.

Alexander Mackenzie was a hard worker and a smart businessman. He knew how to get along with the Indians and with the rough white men who spent their lives in the woods. All these things made him a good trader, but they also helped with the more important work he was about to begin. In 1789, his company asked him if he could find a way from Lake Athabasca to the Pacific Ocean. Mackenzie was anxious to try.

The lands beyond Lake Athabasca had hardly been explored, but Mackenzie had an idea about how to get to the Pacific. With a party of white men and Indians in June 1789, he traveled upstream on the Slave River, which runs south into Lake Athabasca from Great Slave Lake. At Great Slave Lake the men turned west, into a broad, fast river that had no name. This was the river that Mackenzie believed would take him to the sea.

And so it did—but to the wrong sea! After 300 miles,

the great river turned to the north. From that point it flowed for almost 800 miles more, through land so far north that no trees grew there. This was called the *tundra*, and it was the land of caribou and musk oxen.

Once the river turned north, Mackenzie knew that his reasoning must have been wrong. This was not the way to the Pacific. But he kept going, curious as to where the river would lead. The current carried the canoes along so swiftly that in less than two weeks, Mackenzie and his men reached the shores of the Arctic Ocean.

The party returned to Lake Athabasca the same way

Mackenzie gazes upon the Arctic Ocean in 1789, the same year he unsuccessfully attempted to reach the Pacific Ocean.

they had come, but now the trip took longer because they paddled their canoes against the river's current. When he got back to Lake Athabasca, Mackenzie talked of his adventures on what he called the Grand River. But it wasn't called that for long! On today's maps, between Great Slave Lake and the Arctic Ocean, the name that appears for this river is Mackenzie.

The greatest explorers, when they fail to find what they are looking for, turn around and try again. That is what Alexander Mackenzie did in the fall of 1792.

This time, he followed a different river from Lake Athabasca—the Peace River, which flows into Athabasca from its source high in the Rocky Mountains. Mackenzie felt that if he followed the Peace River all the way to its source, he could cross the mountains and perhaps find another river that would take him down to the Pacific Ocean.

Mackenzie did not try, as he had done on his first adventure, to make this trip all at once. Instead, he headed up the river to find a good place to build a winter fort. From there he would travel the rest of the way in the spring, when the snow and ice melted.

The ice was gone by the end of the first week of May 1793. Now Mackenzie chose nine men for his crew. Two of them were Indians, who were good hunters and who knew the languages of the Indian tribes that the party might meet. The men and 3,000 pounds of supplies fit into a single birch bark canoe.

The canoe was 25 feet long and almost five feet wide. But it was light enough for two men to carry.

They had to do just that plenty of times. Paddling the canoe against the current was hard enough. But at waterfalls and the dangerous, rocky places called rapids, the only way to move along was to take everything out of the canoe and carry it to the next safe spot on the river. This is called portaging. Once, the men had to portage four times in two miles. For 800 miles they traveled this way, always pushing against the flow of the river.

The days were as hard as we can imagine. Mackenzie and his men started off at three or four o'clock each morning and paddled until dark. They slept on the cold ground, and their main food was something called *pemmican*. The fur-traders had learned how to make this food from the Indians. It was a mixture of dried beef or buffalo meat, fat, and wild berries, mashed together. It doesn't sound very tasty, but it gave the hardworking men a great deal of energy. Sometimes, the Indian hunters would be lucky, and the party would enjoy a feast of fresh, roasted meat.

As careful as the men tried to be with their canoe, the river would sometimes dash it roughly against sharp rocks. Then everyone would have to get out to dry the supplies and patch the canoe with fresh birch bark and the sticky sap of pine trees, called pitch. In this way, the men were better off than many modern explorers. When a motor breaks deep in the woods, it cannot be fixed with tree bark and sap!

They were also lucky in having so strong and brave a leader. At one point, the bank of the river was too steep to climb down after they had carried the canoe and supplies around the rapids. But Mackenzie got to the bottom and helped the men down by letting them climb onto his powerful shoulders.

The hardest part of the trip came after the party had followed the Peace River all the way to its source. They had met an Indian who told them about a river on the other side of the mountains that would take them to the sea. But before they could reach this river, they had to cut a path through the forest with their axes, so they could drag the canoe along with them.

At last, 40 days after leaving their winter camp, they reached the new river. But their troubles were far from over. Four days after they began the easy paddle downstream, they met a group of Indians who told them that going further would be unwise. The Indians told them that farther down the river, fierce tribes lived. These hostile Indians might not let them pass.

Mackenzie hated to turn back, but he listened to what the Indians said. He and his men paddled the canoe back to where a smaller river led west. However, this river was too fast and shallow for the canoe, so they put it in a safe place, ready for their return trip. Then they set out on foot for the coast.

They walked west for more than two weeks, carrying

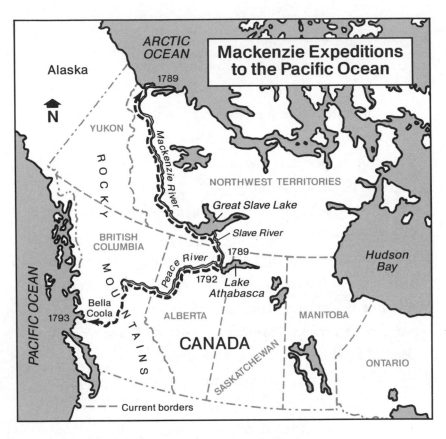

Mackenzie Expeditions to the Pacific Ocean

ARCTIC OCEAN

Alaska

N

YUKON

Mackenzie River

NORTHWEST TERRITORIES

Great Slave Lake

Slave River

BRITISH COLUMBIA

Peace River

1789

1792

Lake Athabasca

Hudson Bay

Bella Coola

1793

ALBERTA

MANITOBA

CANADA

PACIFIC OCEAN

ROCKY

MOUNTAINS

SASKATCHEWAN

ONTARIO

Current borders

their supplies on their backs. Mackenzie was not like some explorers, who had servants carry their heavy loads. He carried his own pack, and it weighed more than 70 pounds.

Alexander Mackenzie reached his goal on July 19, 1793. By then, he and his men had seen that the river they had been walking along emptied into a long, narrow arm of the Pacific Ocean. Before returning, they borrowed an Indian canoe and paddled down to a larger nearby bay. There Mackenzie painted the date on a rock cliff, along with the words, "Alexander Mackenzie, from

Canada, by land." (In those days, "Canada" meant only the eastern part of the country.)

In recent times these words have been painted again in the same place, so they will last. Visitors can see them by boat near the little town of Bella Coola on the coast of British Columbia.

Alexander Mackenzie had become the first man to cross North America by land. He and his party returned safely to their faraway trading posts, and Mackenzie later went back east to become a leading man in the fur

Hardy explorers, Mackenzie and his men rest their eyes on the goal of their long, arduous journey—the Pacific Ocean.

trade and the government of Canada. By the time he died, back home in Scotland in the year 1820, he had been knighted and was Sir Alexander Mackenzie. He wrote a book about his travels, but surely the most important words he ever wrote are those on that rock at the edge of the sea.

One hundred fifty years after Mackenzie's death, the Canadian government honored the great explorer by issuing this 1970 stamp bearing his words.

7

Meriwether Lewis and William Clark

*W*e can hardly imagine the United States suddenly doubling in size or picture the new territory as a largely unexplored wilderness, lived in by a small population of native peoples who had seen very few outsiders. Huge amounts of time, energy, and money, and thousands of carefully trained women and men would be devoted to finding out about the new provinces. If this happened, everyone would talk about it for months, probably years. It would be the biggest news of the century.

We know, of course, that there is no way this could happen, unless we found a new planet that could support human life. The earth we live on has been all but completely discovered, explored, and claimed by its various peoples. But once the United States did double in size, all at the stroke of a pen. The land it

Meriwether Lewis (1774-1809). Three years after leading the famous expedition, Lewis was appointed governor of the Louisiana Territory by President Thomas Jefferson in 1807.

acquired was as wild and fresh, as strange and beautiful and full of promise as anything we can imagine. And the government sent out an expedition to look over this new land—an expedition made up of about three dozen men and one woman. The explorers spent roughly $39,000 on their entire two-year adventure.

The year was 1803. Thomas Jefferson, the brilliant author of the *Declaration of Independence*, was president of the United States. The country at that time was made up of 17 states—the 13 original colonies, plus Vermont, Kentucky, Tennessee, and the new state of Ohio. Future states such as Wisconsin, Michigan, and Illinois were unorganized territories and were thought of as the Far West.

William Clark (1770-1838) loyally served his government, mainly in Indian affairs, for more than three decades following his historic journey.

All of the United States lay east of the Mississippi River.

What about the land to the west of the great river? At the beginning of the 1800s it belonged to Spain, but Spain soon afterwards gave it to France as part of a settlement of affairs between the two countries. Called "Louisiana," the French territory was far larger than the state of Louisiana today. It reached all the way to Canada in the north, and to the west it stretched to include all the land drained by the rivers that flow into the Mississippi. No one knew exactly where its western borders were, since much of western North America had never been explored.

President Jefferson was not comfortable with a vast

French possession lying just west of the United States. He wanted the United States to have the freedom to travel on the Mississippi River and to enjoy free access to the port of New Orleans. He feared that the United States would need to draw closer to England if there should ever be a French threat from the west.

Napoleon, the French emperor, had problems of his own. He feared that in a war with England, he might lose Louisiana. He wanted to see a stronger United States, as a possible rival of England. And he needed money. These reasons led him to offer the entire territory of Louisiana for sale to the United States. The Americans accepted, at a price of 15 million dollars.

Fifteen million dollars was a lot more money in 1803 than it is now, but the price was still incredibly cheap. It came to about three cents an acre, for a territory that included some of the richest farmland in North America. But neither President Jefferson nor anyone else in the United States knew exactly what they had gotten for the price. An expedition would be needed to explore the Louisiana Purchase and to help locate a route to the American fur-trading settlements on the Pacific Coast. Up until then, American traders working along the coast (along the territory that later became Oregon and Washington) had no choice but to send their furs the long distance back to the East Coast by ship.

Jefferson organized his expedition early in 1803. As commander, he chose his own secretary, a 29-year-old army officer named Meriwether Lewis. Lewis was a Virginia neighbor of the president. He was a big, strong man, who was used to a hard life at frontier army posts.

Historians are not sure whether Meriwether Lewis or President Jefferson selected the expedition's second-in-command, William Clark. But both men knew Clark as a tough frontier soldier who had fought Indians, mapped the backcountry, and spied on Spanish forces. He was 33 years old, and like Lewis, he was physically powerful.

President Jefferson gave clear instructions to Lewis and Clark. They were to travel up the Missouri River to its source, and then cross the Rocky Mountains in search of another river that would take them to the Pacific Ocean. If they were lucky, this would be the same river discovered at its mouth in 1792 by an American captain, Robert Gray, and named the Columbia. Such a two-way discovery might help Americans to claim the land all the way to the Pacific. Along the way, Lewis and Clark were to find as much as possible about the Indian tribes they might meet and to take notes on soil, weather, minerals, plants, and animals.

In the America of 1803, just getting to the starting place for such an expedition was a big job. First, Lewis rode on horseback from Washington, D.C., to Pittsburgh, Pennsylvania, where a 55-foot keelboat was being built for the trip. Then, when the boat was finished, the leader had it packed with supplies—guns, ammunition, tools, clothing, medicines, and objects to

Sailing from the Pacific in 1792, Boston seaman Robert Gray (1755-1806) ventured into the Columbia River (named after his ship), only a few years before Lewis and Clark began charting its course.

trade with the Indians. Next he assembled a crew, and began the 1,100-mile trip down the Ohio River to the Mississippi on August 31. Along with the keelboat, which could be rowed, sailed, or pushed with poles, Lewis had two pirogues, large canoes useful with oars or paddles.

Along the way, Lewis picked up Clark in Indiana, and by late November, the two men and their crews were heading up the Mississippi River towards St. Louis, where they were to spend the winter. St. Louis would be the real starting place for the expedition.

Lewis and Clark and their "Corps of Discovery," as it was called, left St. Louis on May 14, 1804. Their three boats carried 41 men in all, mostly soldiers, but also several French backwoodsmen who knew the ways of river travel. Leaving the little frontier settlement behind, they began their struggle against the swift spring currents of the 3,000-mile Missouri River.

Heading west and then north up the wide, muddy Missouri, Lewis and Clark took two months to reach the mouth of the Platte River, near where Omaha, Nebraska, now stands. Along the way, the party of explorers fought clouds of mosquitoes, suffered in the prairie heat, and struggled against currents so strong that they often had to climb out onto the riverbank and pull the boats along with ropes. At night, they ate fresh deer and bear meat, and danced to the tunes of a fiddle one man had brought along.

Near the mouth of the Platte, at a place they named Council Bluffs, Lewis and Clark held their first meeting with the chiefs of a local Indian tribe, the Oto. Speaking through a Frenchman who knew the Indians' language, the Americans gave them tobacco and fishhooks, medals and army jackets, and other things designed to show them the cleverness and power of the new masters of this land. As President Jefferson had instructed Lewis and Clark, they did their best to win the Indians' loyalty. They repeated the ceremony of speeches and gift giving whenever they came upon a new tribe. Farther up river, though, they met a branch of the Sioux nation called the Teton. The Teton Sioux thought little of the presents and for a while threatened not to let the white men pass. But they finally managed to get through without any fighting.

Now, with autumn coming, Lewis and Clark were in the high plains. The land was alive with buffalo, wolves, mule deer, and the fast, antelope-like creature called the pronghorn. The men had plenty of food, but they needed shelter for the winter. During the long months when the Missouri was frozen, the American party stayed at a fort they had built near the villages of the Mandan people, in what is now North Dakota. They had pushed their strong wooden boats more than 1,600 miles.

Lewis and Clark and their Corps spent a winter among the Mandans. Hunting for meat took up much of the men's time. The expedition leaders found out as much as they could from the Indians about the lands that lay ahead. Lewis and Clark also tried to draw maps that would help them in the spring. Perhaps the most pleasant part of the long winter stopover came on New Year's Day, when the Mandans watched wide-eyed as the white men danced to their fiddle.

The Corps was able to head out onto the river again on April 7, 1805. This time, they left the heavy keelboat behind and instead took six smaller boats they had built, along with the two pirogues. Lewis and Clark also added several members to the expedition—two French trappers, who could help with the languages of the Indian tribes up river, and Sacagawea, the young wife of one of these men. Sacagawea was a Shoshoni, and the Shoshoni were one of the tribes that lived farther west.

Lewis and Clark greet the Mandan Indians on the banks of the Missouri River.

Along with Sacagawea came the Corps' youngest member—her baby who had been born during the winter.

On this trek westward, the Lewis and Clark party were sometimes sailors, sometimes oarsmen, and sometimes simply tired men pulling their boats along with ropes. Everything depended on the wind. For four months, the Corps struggled up the wild Missouri, through the far northern plains of what are now North Dakota and Montana. At one point, they had to unload the boats and carry everything around an enormous series of waterfalls. They even had to lug the boats on wagons over the high ground. The place is not forgotten. The city of Great Falls, Montana, stands at this spot today.

Up the river from the falls, the Missouri River grew narrower. The river's current, and the current of the smaller streams that flowed into it, grew faster. (The swift waterways were being fed by the melting snows of the Rocky Mountains, or the Rockies.) The prairies were behind the Corps of Discovery now. Ahead lay the trip through the mountains and the land of the Shoshoni.

Lewis and Clark followed the Missouri to one of its source rivers, which they named Jefferson after the president. Heading as far as they could into the mountains, the Corps reached a point where they had to leave their boats behind. Now, the key to the expedition's success would be meeting with the Shoshoni, who could show the way over the mountains and provide the Corps with horses.

When the Shoshoni appeared, both sides felt tension. This tribe knew nothing of white people. But there, among these strange visitors from the East, the Shoshoni saw one of their own tribe. If Sacagawea had not been with the Corps, Lewis and Clark might never have crossed the mountains before winter—if at all.

Even after trading for horses and finding Shoshoni who would serve as guides, Lewis and Clark could by no means be sure of reaching a river path to the Pacific before the early snows of the high country set in. From the time of their August crossing of the Rockies at Lemhi Pass, along today's Montana-Idaho border, they traveled for two months to find that long-sought river. By way of the Snake River, they finally reached the Columbia. It was October 16, 1805, and they were 3,700 miles from St. Louis. Best of all, they were out of the mountains.

Now the expedition traveled by dugout canoes, which they made by cutting down huge trees and hollowing them out with fire and axes, Indian-style. Along the way they met Indians who thought they were men from the sun and who were afraid until they saw Sacagawea and her baby. But these Indians lived by fishing for salmon—a fine sign, since salmon swam up river from the Pacific!

The Columbia is a wild river, and steering the dugouts with the current was no easy matter. The Corps and Sacagawea had to take long, hard detours on land (called "portages") around dangerous rapids. But with the coming of November, something happened that lifted everyone's spirits: they saw the rising and falling of the ocean's tide upon the river. By November 16, the Corps was camped on the great bay that forms the mouth of the Columbia River. From there, Lewis and Clark invited all who wished to do so to hike with them to a nearly cliff and look out upon the Pacific Ocean.

The story of the expedition, of course, was only half done. There would be a winter camp along the coast, and a year's dangerous travel back the way the Corps had come. Lewis and Clark still had to finish with their

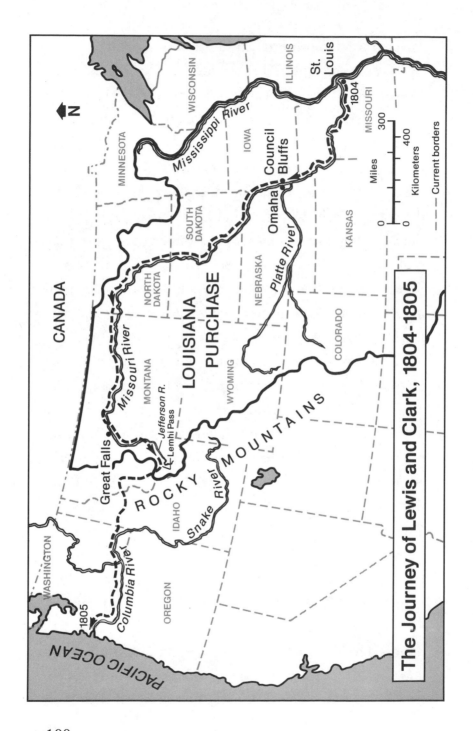

The Journey of Lewis and Clark, 1804-1805

mapmaking and note-taking, all of which would make up a report that met President Jefferson's every expectation, and which still makes fine reading today. And in the years to come, the leaders of the United States and other countries would have to decide who really owned the land between the farthest reaches of the Louisiana Purchase and the sea. (The United States got Oregon and Washington, while England—and later Canada—got British Columbia, farther north.)

But the wondrous part was over. Never again would the continent look so fresh and new as it had to Lewis and Clark.

Lewis and Clark take a much-deserved rest by the mouth of the Columbia River, after their long westward trek. Painted by famous American artist Frederic Remington (1861-1909)

Teacher, surveyor, explorer, soldier, and politician John Charles Frémont sits deep in thought.

8
John Charles Frémont

"*E*very large city in the West was originally my camp."

The man who spoke those words was John Charles Frémont, whose well-deserved nickname was "The Pathfinder." No one has more places in the American West named after him—Fremont counties in Wyoming, Idaho, and Colorado; Fremont Peak in Wyoming; Fremont Glacier in Washington State; the Fremont River in Utah; and the city of Fremont, California, along with more than 100 other "Fremonts" on the map. John Charles Frémont was one of the first explorers to visit and map the vast spaces between the prairies and the Pacific Coast, and he did as much as any person to bind California to the United States.

John Charles Frémont was born in Savannah, Georgia, in 1813, and grew up in Charleston, South Carolina. His father, who died when the boy was only five, was French. (That is the reason for the accent mark over the "e" in Frémont's name.) Years later, when Frémont ran for president of the United States, his enemies used the foreign-looking name to try to prove that Frémont had been born outside the United States. By law, an American president must be born in the United States.

Frémont's widowed mother was poor, and the boy went to work when he was 13 as a clerk for a lawyer. In this job, he learned surveying, or carefully marking where one piece of land ends and another begins. John Charles's intelligence impressed the lawyer, who paid the boy's way through school. Besides his regular studies, John was interested in nature and in adventure stories.

John Charles Frémont grew up healthy and strong, fit for the sort of life he enjoyed reading about. His first adult job was as a teacher, but it was still an adventure. He gave lessons on shipboard to men studying to be naval officers, and sailed as far as South America. Next, he took a job that prepared him for his life's work. Working with an army engineer, he helped survey a new railroad line through Indian territory in the western Carolinas. In 1838, when he was 25, Frémont was made a lieutenant in a special branch of the United States Army in charge of surveying new routes for wagon

Frémont began his exploration of the western United States in 1838, under the direction of Joseph Nicollet (1786-1843).

trains and railroads. America was headed west, and it needed well-marked paths to follow.

During 1838 and 1839, Frémont explored the northern Great Plains, north of the Missouri River and west of the Mississippi, on an expedition led by the French-American scientist Joseph Nicollet. Throughout this journey, Frémont polished his skills as a mapmaker and observer of nature, learned about the Indian tribes of the prairie, and met the fur-trappers and "mountain men" who would later help him on his own wilderness expeditions.

In the 1830s, America west of the Mississippi was an almost completely uncharted frontier. Lewis and Clark had reached the Pacific by way of the Missouri and

Columbia rivers, and a few other explorers had wandered west of the Rocky Mountains, but no settlers had yet followed in their paths. There were fur-trading posts in the far Northwest, and small communities such as San Francisco along the coast of California, which still belonged to Mexico. Anyone wishing to travel to these places from the eastern United States went by ship, either all the way around South America or by way of Central America with a land crossing at Panama or Nicaragua. (There was no Panama Canal.) Train travel was something completely new, even in the East. A coast-to-coast railroad would not be built for another 30 years. Explorers like Nicollet and Frémont had to learn about the vast West, its riches and its dangers, before settlers could cross this land by wagon.

Returning from the West, Frémont spent the next three years in Washington, D.C., working on the notes and maps from the Nicollet expedition. During this time, he married Jessie Benton, daughter of the powerful Missouri senator, Thomas Hart Benton. At first the wedding was kept secret, since Senator Benton had been so opposed to his daughter marrying a poor young army officer that he had even had Frémont sent on a three-month expedition to Iowa. But the old senator came to accept Frémont. After all, the two men shared an important goal: the exploration and settlement of the West.

In 1842, Frémont was given a chance to lead an expedition of his own. The army wanted to build a string

Frémont's marriage to Jessie Benton (1824-1902), daughter of a five-term Missouri senator, helped to secure U.S. government support for his explorations. Frémont's father-in-law, Thomas Hart Benton (1782-1858), favored development of the West and brought powerful political influence toward that goal.

of forts from St. Louis, Missouri, to Wyoming, and chose the 29-year-old adventurer for the task of finding the best route along which to set up the new posts.

Frémont left St. Louis in early May 1842, and headed up the Missouri River to the Platte River, which flows through Nebraska on its way down from its sources in the Rocky Mountains. The Platte was mostly too shallow for boat travel, so the Frémont party followed the stream on horseback and on foot, with mules carrying supplies. In all, 21 mountain men made the trip. Of the many supplies that were packed along on an expedition like this, and on Frémont's later journeys, perhaps the most valuable "equipment" was the knowledge these crafty trappers possessed about wilderness survival, and the Indian tribes they would meet along the way. One of the trappers, Kit Carson, became as well-known as any of the explorers of the West.

Frémont led his men to Fort Laramie, Wyoming, an army post built several years earlier. He had been warned of hostile tribes in the mountain territory to the west, but he decided to push on instead of staying at the fort. His goal was the Wind River range of mountains, along the Continental Divide. The Divide is the height of land, in the Rockies, from which all rivers to the east of the mountains flow into the Atlantic Ocean or the Gulf of Mexico, and all those to the west flow into the Pacific.

Lucky enough not to have had any trouble with the Indians, Frémont reached the Wind River range just

Kit Carson (1809-1868) became famous after his work with Frémont. He led a successful military career, mainly fighting Indians in and around New Mexico. Carson had earned the rank of general at the end of the Civil War.

ahead of a more dangerous enemy—the snow and cold of early autumn. He climbed one of the highest mountains, which still bears the name he gave it—Fremont Peak.

Frémont returned to the Platte by way of the Sweetwater River. Here, on the Platte, he made the biggest mistake of his first expedition—he tried to take a portable rubber boat through rapids. The boat turned over in the raging water, and Frémont and two companions were lucky not to drown. But he lost a lot of valuable equipment. The accident showed a negative side of

Frémont's character. He was brave, but he sometimes took foolish risks.

The return trip was made safely, and by October 1, the party was back in St. Louis. Although much of the territory he had covered had already been visited by a few white men, the government was satisfied because of all the new information Frémont had brought about distances, waterways, and possible trail routes. Frémont was also satisfied, but still restless. Atop Frémont Peak, he had looked west and seen how much more land there was to explore.

Back in Washington, Frémont heard plenty of talk about California. Should the United States try to buy the territory? Was there danger that another country would take it from Mexico? Could there be a war between the United States and Mexico? The government thought that this would be a good time to explore the West beyond the Rocky Mountains, all the way to the Pacific. Frémont was the man to do it. After only a year's rest from his last expedition, Frémont once again started out from St. Louis. On this trip, Frémont took along Kit Carson and other mountain men, as well as two Indian guides. The party followed the Kansas River west from the Missouri. They made their way across Kansas and eastern Colorado, heading up into the corner of Wyoming Frémont had explored earlier. But they crossed the Rockies at a point farther south than Fremont Peak. This was South Pass, where in later years wagon trains using the Oregon Trail would cross the great mountain range.

As they had been before, Frémont and his men were lucky in their dealings with the Indians. A close call came on the prairie, when some Cheyenne and Arapaho began to attack the white men's camp. But the Indians had made a mistake—they thought they were attacking another tribe!

The Frémont party visited the Great Salt Lake and explored it in a rubber boat. As they moved west into the vast expanse that Frémont named the Great Basin, the men began to run low on food. At different times they ate skunk and sea gulls, and once killed a horse for its meat. Finally, they were able to buy food from British traders at Fort Hall, on Idaho's Snake River.

Now winter was coming. By late November, the expedition was on the Columbia River, near the Pacific coast in Oregon. Frémont had done all that had been asked of him, and he could have turned back. Instead, he chose to push south instead of east. He took his men south through Oregon and Nevada, where he saw the rugged Sierra Nevada rising to the west. On the other side was Mexico's California. Frémont decided to cross the mountains.

This was a brave but foolish thing to do. The time was January of 1844. The snow in the mountains was so deep that horses sank up to their ears. During the four weeks the party trudged westward across the high peaks, the men had to eat many of their horses and mules, and even their dog. (Only 33 of 67 horses and mules survived the difficult journey.) Some men went crazy. Two new Indian guides, hired in the valley below, left the party. Luck and nerve kept everyone from dying in the snowy mountains. But finally, Frémont and his band looked down into the valley of the Sacramento River. California! Here they would rest at a ranch owned by a Swiss settler named Sutter. Then they began a 500-mile trek down the warm central valley of California and across the desert to where Las Vegas, Nevada, now stands.

In the desert, Frémont's men suffered their only Indian attack of the expedition, when Paiutes killed one of the party's guides. From then on, Frémont took extra care in the territory of the southwest tribes and reached the safety of a Colorado fort at the beginning of July. From there, another month's travel took the men to St. Louis.

For the rest of the year 1844, Frémont and his wife worked on his report. When it was printed, everyone agreed that he deserved the name "Pathfinder." He had covered 3,500 miles, and his maps and descriptions answered many questions about western geography. He even brought back samples of unknown plants. But Frémont was not ready to retire forever to the East. He still felt the call of the Far West.

By the summer of 1845, Frémont was setting out from Kansas City, Missouri, with 74 men. Using routes different from the second expedition, the party headed

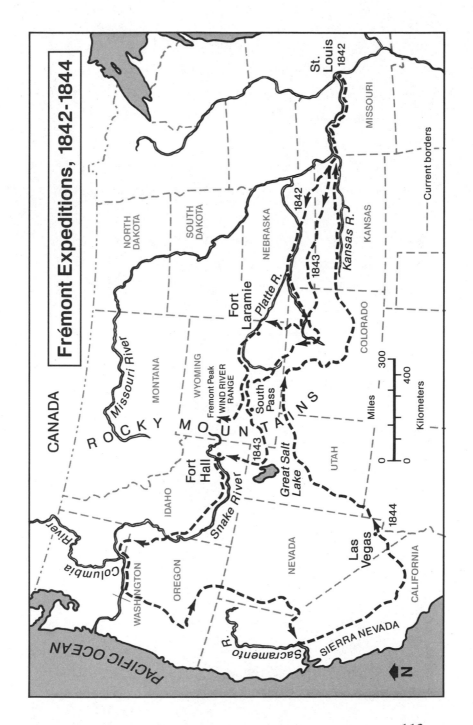

Frémont Expeditions, 1842-1844

across the prairies, the Rockies, and the Great Basin, and crossed the Sierra Nevada before winter set in. Once in California, however, Frémont set himself to tasks other than simple exploration. War with Mexico was approaching.

Historians still argue about what sort of secret orders Frémont may have had, but clearly he soon became involved in the American effort to take California from Mexico. He teamed up with American settlers rebelling against the Mexicans, and later captured San Jose and Los Angeles. A naval officer who probably shouldn't have made such a decision even named Frémont governor of California! Soon, however, Frémont was back in Washington, D.C. An army general had charged the "governor" with disobeying orders. Frémont went on trial and lost his officer's rank for a time.

John Charles Frémont was one of those men who crowd most of their great achievements into the first part of their lives. He was only 33 when the last of his three most important expeditions ended. After that, his life's adventures were of a different sort, and they were seldom successful. He led two more expeditions to the Pacific, not for the government but for railroad builders, and both were failures. Frémont served as one of the first senators from the new state of California, but many people thought he was too harsh in his antislavery views, and his 1850 bid for re-election failed. Frémont's hatred of slavery, along with his fame as an explorer, helped him to win the 1856 presidential nomination of a new antislavery party, the Republicans. He lost to the Democrat, James Buchanan, but the Republicans won the presidency four years later. In that 1860 election, their candidate was Abraham Lincoln.

Frémont served the North as a general in the Civil War. He was twice given important commands, but he had trouble getting along with other generals and won no great victories. Some supporters wanted him to run for president again in 1864, but he did not want to try to take the nomination from Lincoln.

After the war, Frémont tried to get rich in the business of building railroads. All he did, however, was lose the money he had made in the California gold rush,

Union General Frémont failed to turn his pathfinding success into battle-field victories.

along with his fine houses and other properties. His last government job was as governor of the Arizona Territory, from 1878 to 1883. He spent his last years in Los Angeles and died while on a trip to New York City in 1890.

We can only wonder how often, during those long years of fame and disappointment that made up the second part of his life, John Charles Frémont wished he were back on top of his mountain in Wyoming, 29 years old and looking out over all the world.

Appearing old and tired, Frémont stands with his wife, Jessie, and their daughter, Lily, in California, the state to which he had contributed so much earlier in his life.

9

Robert Peary
and Matthew Henson

"*T*here is nothing here. Just ice."

That is how the region around the North Pole looked to a Greenland Eskimo named Ootah, who was a member of the first expedition to reach the Pole, in 1909. Ootah, of course, was right. At the top of the world, an explorer can look in any direction and see nothing at all but ice and sky. To the Eskimo, this was simply more of what he knew at home, only more dangerous because no land supports the ice.

Ootah wasn't at all sure why men from the distant south would travel so far to seek an invisible point in this empty white world. But he knew that nothing was more important in the lives of the men he was with. Robert E. Peary and his assistant, Matthew Henson, had worked toward this moment for 20 years.

Amidst the Arctic ice and snow, Matthew Henson's fellow explorers didn't care about the color of his skin.

Robert Edwin Peary, a United States naval officer, was the first man to choose polar exploration as his life's work. He was the leader of eight Arctic expeditions, the last four of which were attempts to reach the North Pole. Matthew Henson, a black man from Maryland, had once been a cabin boy on a sailing ship and was now Peary's most trusted associate. With help from Eskimos such as Ootah, Peary and Henson ended hundreds of years of mystery about what lay at the northernmost part of the world and settled the question of whether a human being could reach the Pole.

Thorough preparation as well as determination characterized Robert Peary's repeated attempts to reach the North Pole.

Once people realized that the earth is a sphere, rotating on an imaginary center point, or axis, the idea of a North and South Pole was understood. The North Pole, for instance, is the point where all lines of longitude in the Northern Hemisphere come together and where the highest point of latitude is reached. The earth is divided into 360 degrees of longitude, with the lines running north and south. Latitude lines run east and west and are also marked by number: zero degrees at the Equator, with the numbers increasing to 90 degrees at the poles. To reach the North Pole, then, an explorer or a "globe-gazer" has to follow a longitude line to 90 degrees north latitude. (Each degree of latitude equals 60 nautical miles. Nautical miles are slightly larger than the miles we use on road maps.)

As many explorers found out long before Peary and Henson came along, arriving at this longitude and latitude is easier said than done. An explorer can sail a ship only so far north before it becomes locked in ice. Today, strong steel icebreakers can slice through the frozen polar seas, but shifting ice could trap and crush old-fashioned wooden ships.

Land travel in the far north is just as difficult. Snow and ice cover the land closest to the Pole for much of the year. Before the age of airplanes and snowmobiles, the only way to get around in such a hostile climate was the way the Eskimos did—by dog sled.

Finally, as Robert Peary discovered when he began exploring the Arctic, there is no land anywhere near the North Pole. Before Peary, no one knew for sure how far north Greenland extended. When he discovered its northern shores, he realized that the North Pole was still about 500 miles away. The only other land masses within 1,000 miles of the Pole are the barren islands that lie to the north of Canada, Russia, and Norway.

The North Pole lies at the center of the Arctic Ocean, a body of water up to 15,000 feet deep, covered with shifting masses of ice. The ice, which is only five to seven feet deep in many places, is bulged and broken in a way that makes sled travel very dangerous.

Robert Peary chose a difficult goal for himself and spent most of his life reaching it. Peary was born in Pennsylvania, in 1856, and grew up in Maine. He graduated from college with a degree in civil engineering, which he used to design piers and other structures after joining the United States Navy in 1881. In 1884, the Navy sent him to Nicaragua, where a crew was looking for a possible route for a canal between the Atlantic and Pacific oceans. Some time after he returned, in the following year, he began reading about a quite different part of the world—Greenland.

In 1886, Peary asked for six months leave from his Navy duties and sailed to Greenland aboard a whaling ship. There, he and another young man with a taste for adventure traveled deep into the huge island's interior. Pulling his sled across the Greenland ice, Peary decided once and for all that Arctic exploration would be his life.

First, though, he had to make another trip to Nicaragua. Peary did, after all, still have to take orders from the Navy. Back in Washington, he got together his equipment for the arctic adventure. One of the things he needed was a new sun helmet and, when he went into a store to buy it, the shopkeeper introduced him to his

Peary, a graduate of Bowdoin College in Maine, brought a strong scientific and technical background to his explorations.

21-year-old helper, Matt Henson. Peary had been telling the shopkeeper that he was looking for a *valet*, or servant, to go with him to Nicaragua. Young Henson, he was told, might be just the man for the job.

Matt Henson knew about a lot more than stocking shelves in a clothing store. He had left home at 12 and gone to sea as a cabin boy. A kind captain had taught him seamanship, and introduced him to books on a great many other subjects. On the trip to Nicaragua, Peary quickly realized that such a bright young man should not be stuck with the job of a valet. He could do much more than look after his boss's clothes and living quarters. In Nicaragua, Peary gave Henson greater responsibilities, as part of his surveying crew.

Though they first worked together in the hot, steamy climate of Nicaragua, Peary and Henson later devoted themselves to mastering the frozen north.

That began two decades of teamwork. As the years went by, Peary took longer leaves of absence from the Navy, so that he could continue his Arctic explorations. Each time, he took Matt Henson along as a member of his crew. The two took four more expeditions to Greenland, during which Peary discovered the northern limits of the island and proved that it was not a continent stretching to the North Pole and beyond.

On these Greenland expeditions Peary learned that the best way to travel on the Arctic ice was to imitate the Eskimos. He used Eskimo dog sleds, wore Eskimo furs, and built Eskimo igloos that kept him and his men warmer than the tents other explorers used. All the while, both Matt Henson and Peary were getting to know the North. Henson became friends with the Eskimos, and learned to drive a dog sled as well as any of them.

In 1898, Peary sailed to Greenland on the first of his attempts to reach the North Pole itself. He and Henson, along with the rest of his crew, spent four years in the Arctic. But Peary never got closer than 360 miles from the Pole. On a new expedition in 1905-1906, he trimmed this distance down to 174 miles. By now, the explorer was 50, and he must have realized that he would not have many more chances to try for his difficult prize. And with each failure, getting people to give money to support the expensive expeditions became harder.

With every step that brought him closer to the North Pole, though, Peary had been learning. He knew that the best stepping-off place for the final sled drive across the frozen Arctic Ocean was not Greenland, but Canada's Ellesmere Island. He learned that winter, not summer, was the best time for polar travel, because the Arctic ice was firmer. If he left too late in the year, drifting ice could strand him at sea. And he learned he had no more useful comrade than Matt Henson.

In July 1908, Peary's ship *Roosevelt* sailed once more from New York. Its destination was the northern shore of Ellesmere Island. There, Peary set up his base camp—and there, on March 1, 1909, he began his final push to the North Pole. He had with him 19 sleds, 133 dogs, and 23 men. Of the men, 17 were Eskimos, and six, including Matt Henson, were Americans.

Peary did not plan on taking all these men and dogs to the North Pole with him. His style of traveling called for the group to get smaller and smaller as it got closer to the Pole. Support parties would turn back as they were no longer needed, leaving a fast, easily managed party of six men, five sleds, and 40 dogs. Peary, Henson, Ootah, Egingwah, Seegloo, and Ookeah would be the first men to stand on top of the world.

When the last support party dropped back, Peary was only 133 nautical miles from the Pole. The date was April 2, and the temperature was 25 degrees below zero Fahrenheit. "A fine marching morning," Peary called it. But what a march! In some places, 50-foot-high "pressure ridges," caused by huge sheets of ice buckling together, stood before the crew. In other places, because of gaps of open water called "leads," the men had to drive their 12-foot sleds toward safe crossing places and lose precious time. At one point, Peary had to take his sleds from one floating cake of ice to another, balancing to keep the ice from tipping. Both Peary and Henson fell into the frigid water—Ootah pulled Henson to safety—

and both were grateful for the heavy bearskin clothing that protected them. Night found the men so exhausted that they could barely build igloos for shelter. But after they did, Peary wrote, their wind-bitten faces "pained us so that we could hardly go to sleep." The air "was as keen and bitter as frozen steel."

Running his sled ahead of Peary's, Matt Henson reached a spot he believed was close to the North Pole, if not the Pole itself. When Peary arrived, he took a reading with his instruments. He could not be perfectly sure, since the navigational instruments of 1909 were not precisely accurate, but the instruments showed that they were within three miles of their goal! Just to be sure, they sledded ahead to a point where the instruments said they were past the North Pole; then they headed south again. Satisfied, Peary drove his dogs back and set up his polar camp. The party raised the American flag at the Pole on April 6, 1909.

Peary, Henson, and the Eskimos raced back to Ellesmere Island, fearing that the Arctic summer and its thawing ice might overtake them. Their luck held, and they reached their base camp in an amazing 16 days. Peary could hardly wait to tell the world that he had finally reached the North Pole! As soon as he could get his ship free of the ice, he steamed south to the nearest telegraph station, thousands of miles away in Labrador.

Peary sent his message, then got another message that shocked and saddened him. Another explorer, Dr.

Polar explorers often came upon scenes of awesome beauty—and potential terror.

Peary and Henson Expedition to the North Pole, 1909

RUSSIA

RUSSIA

Arctic Circle

ARCTIC OCEAN

NORWAY

North Pole

Ellesmere Island

ICELAND

GREENLAND

Alaska

Miles
0   600

0   800
Kilometers

CANADA

Frederick Cook, claimed to have reached the North Pole nearly a year before Peary.

Peary was sure that Cook was lying. The man had lied before, about being the first to climb Mt. McKinley in Alaska. (Today, most people agree that Peary was really first to the Pole.) Cook did not have the notes and figures to back up his claim. But instead of parties and parades, Peary came home to several years of working to prove his case. For some reason, people wanted to believe Cook. Peary even had to fight to win promotion to admiral and to receive his Navy pension.

Years of controversy followed Peary's successful expedition. Many people doubted Peary had reached the North Pole first; others criticized him for having made the trip with a black man.

Even when people did believe Peary, they criticized him for taking a black man to the North Pole, instead of a white. But the explorer stuck by his friend. Of all the Americans on his expedition, he said, "Henson was the best man I had with me for this kind of work."

The hard years in the Arctic, along with the bitterness of the fight with Cook, made an old man of Peary. He died in 1920, at the age of 63. But Henson had a long life ahead of him. Racial prejudice kept him in a low-paying government job, and some writers even said he had been only Peary's "servant." Eventually, however, people recognized his contributions. Groups such as the National Geographic Society, as well as President Dwight Eisenhower himself, understood how important Henson had been to Peary, and honored him. Henson was even made a member of the Explorer's Club. He died in 1955, and was buried in a simple grave in New York City. In 1988 though, the United States government moved his body to Arlington National Cemetery in Washington, D.C. There, Matthew Henson rests beside Robert E. Peary, comrades to the end and beyond.

Matthew Henson finally received the credit he deserved for his contributions to polar exploration, including recognition from the Explorer's Club, which honored him late in his life.

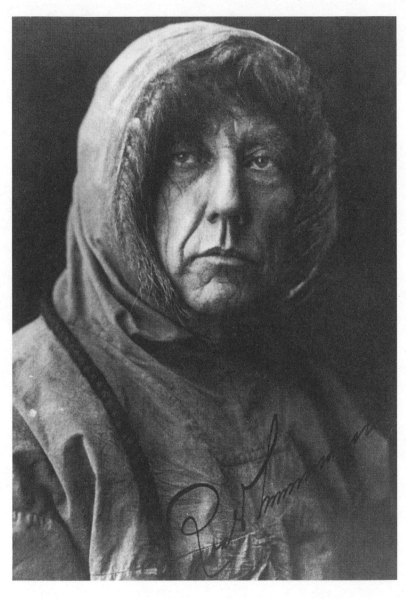

*Like many Norwegians, Roald Amundsen chose to lead a life
at sea. None, however, would earn the international fame
and admiration from his countrymen that Amundsen did.*

132

10
Roald Amundsen

Often, the person who scores a great success in the world of exploration is only one of a long line of people who have tried, and failed to achieve the same thing. That person's victory stands alongside many defeats, and even tragedies.

In one of history's most famous exploratory adventures, one man reached a long-sought goal and returned safely, as another met death after reaching the same prize one month too late to be first. This is the story of the race to the South Pole. The tragedy was that of Robert Scott, and the victory was that of Roald Amundsen—the first man to reach the bottom of the world.

The continent of Antarctica, where the South Pole is located, is as large as Europe and Australia put

The world gained much scientific and geographical knowledge from the Antarctic explorations of British naval officer Robert Scott (1868-1912).

together. Far from other lands and surrounded by a dangerous, ice-choked sea, it was the last of the continents to be discovered. Until modern scientists began to set up camps on its ice, no one had ever lived there. The reason is simple: a layer of ice and snow, in some places two miles thick, covers nearly all of Antarctica. The temperature can drop to 100 degrees below zero Fahrenheit, and fierce blizzards rage in every season of the year.

At the beginning of the twentieth century, the South Pole was one of the few places on earth that explorers had never reached. (The Americans, Peary and Henson, attained the North Pole in 1909, as related in the previous chapter.) The South Pole is the southernmost place on earth. When an explorer stands at the South Pole, every direction is north.

Ernest Shackleton, an Englishman, made the first serious attempt to reach the South Pole in 1907-1909. Running low on food, Shackleton's party had to give up their expedition and return to the seacoast when they were only 97 miles from the Pole. Within three years, however, two more expeditions made the attempt: a group led by the Norwegian Roald Amundsen, and another by English Captain Robert Scott.

Roald Amundsen knew a great deal about polar exploration. As a teenager, he had already decided that this was how he would spend his life—he even slept with the windows open during the cold Norwegian winters to prepare himself. In his early twenties, he took long trips across the empty, snow-covered wilds of his native country.

Amundsen sailed as an officer on an expedition to the Antarctic in 1897. In 1903, he took charge of a voyage that would make him famous. Sailing a 70-foot fishing boat called the *Gjøa*, Amundsen and his crew became the first men to navigate the entire length of the

Ernest Shackleton (1874-1922), his party, and his ship faced daunting obstacles during their unsuccessful attempt to reach the South Pole.

Northwest Passage—the dangerous, almost icebound, route that winds between the northern Canadian mainland and Canada's Arctic islands. Since the men had to camp for three winters while waiting for the passage to thaw, the trip lasted until 1906. Along the way, Amundsen located the position of the North Magnetic Pole, which is the place compass needles point to in the Northern Hemisphere.

By 1910, the 38-year-old Amundsen was ready to attempt the South Pole. With 19 men and 100 husky dogs, he set sail for Antarctica in his ship *Fram* in August of that year.

Amundsen was a firm believer in careful planning. Before leaving Norway, he studied maps and reports of the Antarctic coast and decided exactly where his main camp would be. He made sure that every piece of equipment would be perfect for its job. As for the dogs, his planning went even further and resulted in a decision we might not like to read about today. However, Amundsen felt that this decision was vital to the success of the expedition.

Amundsen's ship, Fram, *is loaded with dogs and supplies.*

Amundsen knew that the farther he and his men traveled across the Antarctic ice, the lighter the loads on their sleds would become. The men would be using up the food they had brought, but they would still need food to finish the trip to the South Pole and return to their ship. Since lighter sleds needed fewer dogs to pull them, Amundsen planned to solve two problems at once: One by one, his men would kill 40 dogs. Then the men and the remaining dogs would eat the meat. Amundsen did not like to have to do this, but his first concerns were for the survival of his men and the success of the expedition. And in those days, dogs were still the best means of transportation in polar regions. He had learned this from the Eskimos during those winters he had spent in the Canadian Arctic waiting for the Northwest Passage to thaw.

Amundsen and his party set out for the Pole from a spot called the Bay of Whales, on Antarctica's Ross Ice Shelf, on October 18, 1911. Meanwhile, however, another polar explorer was only three weeks away from beginning his own trek towards the South Pole. This was Captain Robert Scott, who had camped nearly 400 miles away on the other side of the ice shelf.

Captain Scott, who was leading a British expedition, had decided upon a means of travel that differed from Amundsen's. He used dogs, but he had also brought along a number of long-haired Siberian ponies to pull his supply sleds. He also had three gasoline-powered motor sleds that ran on tracks. With the ponies, dogs, and machines, Scott would move step by step, setting up bases along the way. Like Amundsen, he would cover the final distance with only a few companions. But Scott's plan for this last stage was different. He and his men would pull their sleds themselves, without dogs, and reach the South Pole on foot.

For Amundsen, everything went according to plan. In the first four days the swift dog sleds covered nearly 90 miles of the roughly 600 miles to the Pole. Amundsen even fixed ropes behind the sleds, so the dogs could tow him and his men along on skis. The hardest part of the journey came when the party reached steep slopes, where they sometimes had to push the sleds to help the dogs, and at *crevasses*, or deep cracks in the snow and ice. If a sled suddenly tipped into a crevasse, dogs and men would plunge to their deaths.

Except for a few days, the weather on Amundsen's southward trip was fine. October is springtime in Antarctica, and by December—when the party was within 100 miles of the Pole—the temperature rose as high as zero degrees Fahrenheit. Amundsen even wrote that the men were sometimes too warm while they were skiing alongside the sleds and had to take off some of their heavy clothes. By December 7, Amundsen's careful planning and good luck with the weather had brought him past the farthest point Shackleton had reached on his earlier expedition. The small group of Norwegians were now farther south than anyone had ever been before.

Captain Scott had a different sort of luck. His motor sleds kept breaking down, and the party abandoned them by the end of the first week. Blizzards sometimes made traveling impossible. The ponies and dogs pulled sleds as far as they could, but the last part of the route Scott had chosen went up a steep glacier, and the animals were no longer of any use. Scott took four men for the final march to the South Pole, and they went off on foot with their sleds. That was on January 4, 1912.

Little did Scott know, while he was preparing for the final push, that he no longer had any hope of being the first to reach the South Pole. Amundsen and his men had spent the second week of December steadily advancing in good weather. During the night of December 13, Amundsen later wrote, he kept waking up with "the same feeling that I can remember as a little boy on the night before Christmas Eve." He knew that on the next day, he would receive the greatest gift of his life.

During the last miles of travel by sled and skis on December 14, the worst thing Amundsen's party could think of was approaching the Pole and seeing the British flag flying. They had no way of knowing how Scott had been doing. But as they looked ahead into the Antarctic whiteness, they could see no sign of human occupation. Around three o'clock, Amundsen's sled drivers called "Halt!" together. The distance meters they had set up on their sleds all told the same story: they were at the South Pole.

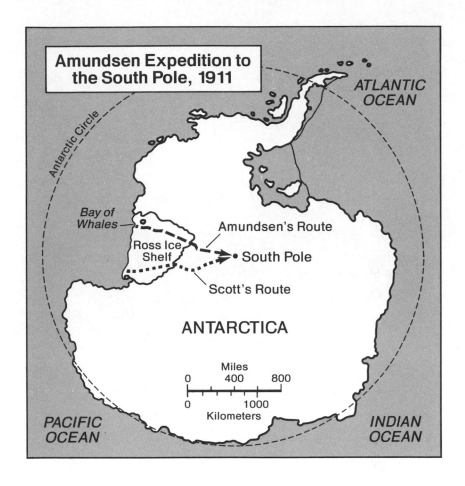

Amundsen Expedition to the South Pole, 1911

ATLANTIC OCEAN

Antarctic Circle

Bay of Whales

Amundsen's Route

Ross Ice Shelf

South Pole

Scott's Route

ANTARCTICA

Miles
0   400   800

0   1000
Kilometers

PACIFIC OCEAN

INDIAN OCEAN

Amundsen's instruments gave the same reading, but just to be sure they had made no mistake and missed by a tiny distance, the men strapped on skis and made a great circle around the spot. Somewhere within the circle, they were certain, lay the invisible object of their quest.

At their camp, Amundsen joined with the others to raise the flag of Norway and to leave a message for the Norwegian king in case anything should happen to them on the way back. They named the spot "*Polheim,*" which is Norwegian for "Pole Home."

Polheim, the Norwegian camp at the South Pole, where Amundsen and his men marked the southernmost point in the world

The five Englishmen arrived at Polheim on January 17, just one month and two days after Amundsen had left. "It is a terrible disappointment," Scott wrote in his diary. But the coming month would be far more terrible. Going back the way they had come, Scott's party met with blizzards and temperatures of 40 degrees below zero Fahrenheit. The Antarctic autumn was coming. The bad weather and poor snow surface made traveling more than six miles a day very difficult. Food and fuel for the camp stove began to run out, and frostbite blackened the men's feet. By the end of February, Scott knew that he and his men were in desperate trouble.

By March 16, two members of the expedition had died: One had fallen on rough glacier ice. The other, who knew his frostbitten feet could not carry him to the base camp, had wandered into a blizzard to die so he would not slow down his companions. On March 29, Scott and his two remaining men put up their tent and crawled into their sleeping bags. The leader wrote in his diary for the last time—"For God's sake look after our people." A search party found the diary, along with the three frozen dead men, eight months later. They

Scott consistently kept a diary through both comfortable and harsh conditions. His last entries showed the world a brave man who knew he was doomed.

were 11 miles from a supply of food and fuel they had stored on the trip south.

Roald Amundsen and his men had the same good luck on their return trip as they had had on their way to the South Pole. They traveled 17 miles a day with their dog sleds, enjoyed fine weather, and had plenty of food. They reached their base camp on January 25, 1912, after a round trip of 99 days and 1,860 miles.

Amundsen lived to have other adventures, including flying over the North Pole in a dirigible airship in 1926. But two years later, as he was flying on a rescue mission in the Arctic, his plane crashed and he lost his life. Like Captain Robert Scott, Roald Amundsen did not seem meant to die in a warm bed.

And even if he had died in bed, he probably would have had the windows open.

Chronology of Explorers
and World Events

1304   **Muhammad ibn-Abdullah ibn-Batuta born in Tangier, Morocco**

1327   **Ibn-Batuta made second trip to Mecca**

1333   **Ibn-Batuta crossed the Asian plains and mountains to reach India**

1337   Outbreak of The Hundred Years War in Europe

1349   **Ibn-Batuta arrived home in Tangier 24 years after his journey began**

1369   **Ibn-Batuta died**

1394   Prince Henry "The Navigator" born

1431   Joan of Arc burned at the stake in Rouen, France

1445   Johann Gutenberg invented the printing press in Mainz, Germany

1460	Prince Henry "The Navigator" died
1469	**Vasco da Gama born**
1488	Bartholomew Dias reached the Cape of Good Hope at Africa's southern tip
1492	Christopher Columbus arrived in America
1497	**Da Gama began his voyage to India**
1498	**Da Gama's ships reached India, ten months after leaving Portugal**
1509	Henry VIII becomes King of England (died 1547)
1519	Ferdinand Magellan began his successful journey to circumnavigate the globe
1524	**Da Gama died in India while serving as royal governor**
1567	**Samuel de Champlain born in Brouage, France**
1603	**Champlain explored Canada's St. Lawrence River**

1608   **Champlain founded the town of Quebec**

1618   The Thirty Years War began in Europe

1620   Pilgrims on the *Mayflower* reached Massachusetts

1629   **Champlain taken prisoner of war and brought to England**

1635   **Champlain died**

1637   **Jacques Marquette born in Laon, France**

1642   English Civil War began (ended 1648)

1673   **Marquette and Louis Joliet began search for the Mississippi River**

1675   **Marquette died**

1728   **James Cook born in Yorkshire, England**

1755   **Cook joined the British Navy**

1764   **Alexander Mackenzie born in Scotland**

1768   Cook left England on the *Endeavor* for new islands in the Pacific

1770   William Clark born

1771   Cook's *Endeavor* returned to England

1773   Cook became the first person to sail across the Antarctic Circle

1774   Meriwether Lewis born

1775   American Revolution began

1775   Cook's ship, *Resolution*, arrived back in England

1776   Cook set out to find the Northwest Passage

1779   Cook died during a skirmish with Hawaiians

1789   French Revolution began

1793   Mackenzie reached the Pacific Ocean by land

1803   United States made the Louisiana Purchase

1804	Lewis and Clark began expedition to map the Louisiana Purchase
1809	Lewis died
1813	John Charles Frémont born in Savannah, Georgia
1815	Napoleon defeated at Waterloo
1820	Mackenzie died
1838	With Joseph Nicollet, Frémont explored the northern Great Plains
1838	Clark died
1844	Frémont crossed Sierra Nevada into California
1856	Robert Peary born in Pennsylvania
1861	American Civil War began (ended 1865)
1868	Matthew Henson born
1872	Roald Amundsen born

1890 Frémont died

1898 Peary and Henson made their first attempt
to reach the North Pole

1909 Peary and Henson reached the North Pole

1911 Amundsen reached the South Pole

1914 World War I began (ended 1918)

1920 Peary died

1928 Amundsen died

1939 World War II began (ended 1945)

1955 Henson died

1969 Astronauts landed on the moon

Bibliography

Armstrong, Joe C.W. *Champlain*. Toronto: Macmillan of Canada, 1987.

Beaglehole, J.C. *The Life of Captain James Cook*. Stanford, CA: Stanford University Press, 1974.

Bishop, Morris. *The Life of Fortitude*. Toronto: McClelland and Stewart, 1963.

Connell, Evan S. *A Long Desire*. New York: Holt, Rinehart and Winston, 1979.

_____. *The White Lantern*. New York: Holt, Rinehart and Winston, 1980.

Defremery C., and B.R. Sanguinetti, eds., *The Travels of Ibn Batuta*. Millwood, N J: Kraus, 1986.

Daniels, Roy. *Alexander Mackenzie and the Northwest*. New York: Barnes and Noble, 1969.

DeVoto, Bernard, ed., *The Journals of Lewis and Clark*. Boston: Houghton and Mifflin, 1953.

Dunn, Ross E. *The Adventures of Ibn-Batuta, a Muslim Traveler of the Fourteenth Century*. Berkeley: University of California Press, 1986.

Egan, Ferol. *Frémont, Explorer for a Restless Nation*. Garden City, NY: Doubleday, 1977.

Hart, Henry Hersch. *Sea Road to the Indies*. New York: Macmillan, 1950.

Herbert, Wally. *The Noose of Laurels: Robert E. Peary and the Race to the North Pole.* New York: Atheneum, 1989.

Huntford, Roland. *The Amundsen Photographs.* New York: Atlantic Monthly Press, 1987.

_____. *Scott and Amundsen.* New York: Putnam, 1980.

Jones, Vincent. *Sail the Indian Sea.* London and New York: Gordon and Cremonesi, 1978.

Kjelgaard, Jim. *The Explorations of Père Marquette.* New York: Random House, 1951.

Lavender, David. *The Way to the Western Sea: Lewis and Clark Across the Continent.* New York: Harper & Row, 1988.

Maclean, Alistair. *Captain Cook.* Garden City, NY: Doubleday, 1972.

Morison, Samuel Eliot. *Samuel de Champlain, Father of New France.* Boston: Little, Brown, 1972.

Parry, J.H. *The Age of Reconnaissance.* Berkeley: University of California Press, 1981.

Pound, Reginald. *Scott of the Antarctic.* New York: Coward-McCann, 1967.

Repplier, Agnes. *Père Marquette: Priest, Pioneer and Adventurer.* Garden City, NY: Doubleday, Doran and Co., 1929.

Robinson, Bradley, with Matthew Henson. *Dark Companion: The Story of Matthew Henson.* Greenwich, CT: Fawcett, 1969.

Rolle, Andrew. *John Charles Frémont: Character of Destiny.* Norman, Oklahoma: University of Oklahoma Press, 1991.

Ronda, James P. *Lewis and Clark Among the Indians.* Lincoln, Nebraska: University of Nebraska Press, 1984.

Savours, Ann, ed., *Scott's Last Voyage, through the Antarctic Camera of Herbert Ponting.* New York: Praeger, 1975.

Sheppe, Walter, ed., *First Man West: Alexander Mackenzie's Journal of His Voyage to the Pacific Coast of Canada in 1793.* Westport, CT: Greenwood Press, 1976.

Spence, Mary Lee and Donald Jackson, eds., *The Expeditions of John Charles Frémont.* Urbana, IL: University of Illinois Press, 1970.

Stefansson, Vilhjalmur, ed., *Great Adventures and Explorations.* New York: The Dial Press, 1952.

Syme, Ronald. *The Travels of Captain Cook.* New York: McGraw-Hill, 1971.

Villiers, Alan. *Captain James Cook.* New York: Scribner, 1967.

Weems, John Edward. *Peary: The Explorer and the Man.* London: Eyre & Spottiswoode, 1967.

Index

158

Photo Credits

Photographs courtesy of Library of Congress: pp. 6, 26, 28, 36, 41, 54, 59, 66, 67, 101, 107 (bottom), 118, 127, 134, 136, 137, 142, 143; *Aramco World*, pp. 12, 20-21; Embassy of the Arab Republic of Egypt, Washington, D.C., p. 15; Royal Embassy of Saudi Arabia, Information Office, Washington, D.C., pp. 18, 19; Based on painting by N. Dance / National Archives of Canada / C-16946, p. 34; Based on painting by John Webber / National Archives of Canada / C-34667, p. 43; Based on painting by N. Dance / National Archives of Canada / C-17726, p. 49; Based on lithograph by Louis C.J. Ducornet / National Archives of Canada / C-6643, p. 50; Based on painting by C.W. Jefferys / National Archives of Canada / C-103059, p. 57; Based on painting by Sheriff Scott / National Archives of Canada / C-33195, p. 64; Based on painting by A. Russell / National Archives of Canada / C-6292, p. 74; Based on drawing by T. Lawrence / National Archives of Canada / C-2146, p. 78; Based on drawing by C.W. Jefferys / National Archives of Canada / C-70230, p.82; Based on drawing by C.W. Jefferys / National Archives of Canada / C-73712, p. 87; Based on painting by J.N. Marchand / National Archives of Canada / C-8486, front cover; Based on drawing by C.W. Jefferys / National Archives of Canada / C-69723, back cover; Minnesota Historical Society, pp. 71, 73, 90, 91, 94, 97, 102, 105, 107 (top), 109, 115, 116; Prairie Du Chien Area Chamber of Commerce, p. 77; Yvonne Sharpe, p. 88; William H. Hobbs Collection, Special Collections Library, University of Michigan, pp. 119, 122, 123, 129, 131, 132.